Kentucky Bucket List Adventure Guide

*Explore 100 Offbeat
Destinations You Must Visit!*

Paul Mckee

Bridge Press
support@bridgepress.org

Please consider writing a review!
Just visit: purplelink.org/review

ISBN: 978-1-955149-46-4

FREE BONUS

Find Out 31 Incredible Places You Can
Visit Next! Just Go To:

purplelink.org/travel

Table of Contents

How to Use This Book

Welcome to your very own adventure guide to exploring the many wonders of the state of Kentucky. Not only does this book lay out the most wonderful places to visit and sights to see in the vast state, but it provides driving directions and GPS coordinates for Google Maps to make exploring that much easier.

Adventure Guide
Sorted by region, this guide offers over 100 amazing wonders found in Kentucky for you to go see and explore. These can be visited in any order, and this book will help you keep track of where you've been and where to look forward to going next. Each portion describes the area or place, what to look for, how to get there, and what you may need to bring along.

GPS Coordinates
As you can imagine, not all of the locations in this book have a physical address. Fortunately, some of our listed wonders are either located within a national park or reserve or are near a city, town, or place of business. For those that are not associated with a specific location, it is easiest to map it using GPS coordinates.

Luckily, Google has a system of codes that converts the coordinates into pin-drop locations that Google Maps is able to interpret and navigate.

Each adventure in this guide will include both the GPS coordinates and general directions on how to find the location.

It is important that you are prepared for poor cell signals. It is recommended that you route your location and ensure that the directions are accessible offline. Depending on your device and the distance of some locations, you may need to travel with a backup battery source.

About Kentucky

Known as the Bluegrass State, Kentucky was admitted to the Union as the 15th state in 1792. Approximately 14,000 years ago, Native American tribes like the Yuchi, Shawnee, Cherokee, and Chickasaw roamed the area along with mammoths and other large game animals. The first permanent white settlement in the state was founded in 1774, and future settlements were founded by pioneers James Harrod and Daniel Boone.

Prior to becoming a state, part of present-day Kentucky was actually part of Virginia, but that area did not believe that its interests were being properly represented, so it broke away from Virginia to become its own state. In 1818, the western part of Kentucky was purchased from the Chickasaw tribe to become the full state we know today.

The name "Kentucky" has a cloudy origin. Some experts believe it came from the Wyandot name, "Kah-ten-tah-teh" (Land of Tomorrow), while others believe it's from the Shawnee name, "Kain-tuck-ee" (At the Head of the River), or the Mohawk name, "Kentucke" (Among the Meadows). It is fairly clear that the name came from a Native American language, but experts do not agree on which one.

Many famous explorers, inventors, and political leaders hail from Kentucky, including presidents Abraham Lincoln and Zachary Taylor. Other famous Kentuckians include Colonel Harland Sanders (founder of Kentucky Fried Chicken), Henry Clay, Mary Todd Lincoln, Daniel Boone, James Harrod, Duncan Hines, Hunter S. Thompson, Ned Beatty, George Clooney, Rosemary Clooney, Billy Ray Cyrus, Johnny Depp, the Judds, Jennifer Lawrence, Loretta

Lynn, Nick Lachey, Muhammad Ali, Darrell Waltrip, and Michael Waltrip, among many others.

As you'll soon see, Kentucky is also full of natural attractions, parks, and other spectacular sites, including Fort Knox, the Louisville Slugger Museum, Churchill Downs, and the Country Music Highway. Horse lovers, in particular, will enjoy many attractions around the state.

Landscape and Climate

Bordered by seven states (Indiana and Ohio in the north, West Virginia and Virginia in the east, Tennessee in the south, and Missouri and Illinois in the west), Kentucky consists of six distinct geographical regions. To the east is the Mountain Region, which is characterized by the Appalachian Mountains, forests, high ridges, and deep valleys. In the west, you'll find the Knobs region, where there are hundreds of hills called monadnocks.

The Bluegrass Region, located in the center of the Knobs, is known for the bluish-green grass that is native to the area. You'll also find caves, springs, hills, and sinkholes here, which were created by the erosion of limestone. Continuing west, you'll come across the Pennyroyal Region, which is named after a plant native to the region. Caves, trees, lakes, and rocky terrain distinguish this region from the others.

The Western Coalfield Region is situated in the middle of the Pennyroyal Region and is marked by 4,680 square miles of coal. The area is hilly and is home to the John James Audubon State Park. Finally, the Jackson Purchase, which is the western part of the state that was purchased in 1818, is characterized by lakes, ponds, and swamps.

The weather in Kentucky is usually mild and moderate, but the northern regions can become cold in the winter. The southern regions can be hot and humid, with sudden thunderstorms in the summer. Across the state, the temperature averages 87 degrees in the summer, and lows can reach 23 degrees in the winter. Snow and ice are common, especially in the northern parts of the state.

Visitors flock to Kentucky in the spring and fall when the humidity is at its lowest but the temperatures are still warm. In the spring, the wildflowers bloom, and the bluegrass fields shimmer with color. In the fall, the foliage on the trees turns red, orange, yellow, and gold, making landscapes stunningly picturesque. Summer is also a popular time for visitors, particularly for those who enjoy a multitude of water sports on one of the many lakes in the state.

76 Falls

Located along Indian Creek in Clinton County, Kentucky, 76 Falls is an 84-foot waterfall that is tucked away in a cove of Lake Cumberland. It can be reached by foot and by boat, and the drop pool is a wonderful place to spend a relaxing day. Surrounded by rocky cliffs, 76 Falls is one of the most picturesque waterfalls in Kentucky, especially in the fall when the leaves are changing colors. There is also a foot trail that leads to the road above the falls, where there is a small parking area so that people passing by can stop and catch a glimpse of this spectacular waterfall. In the summer, the cove can be crowded with boats, and the area is known as a party spot, so choosing to visit during the week is a better option to get a more peaceful experience.

Best Time to Visit: The spring is the best time to visit to see the waterfall flowing at its most powerful, but the best pictures can be taken in the fall with the changing foliage.

Pass/Permit/Fees: There is no fee to visit 76 Falls.

Closest City or Town: Albany, Kentucky

How to Get There: From Albany, take US-127 N. Continue onto State Hwy 734 to reach State Hwy 3062. The falls are in 1.8 miles.

GPS Coordinates: 36.78297° N, -85.12617° W

Did You Know? While many people believe that 76 Falls is named for its height, it's actually named for the nearby community of Seventy-Six, Kentucky. The waterfall is actually about eight feet higher than its name!

Diamond Caverns

Discovered in 1859, Diamond Caverns is named for the sparkling calcite formations that resemble diamonds. The cave was immediately developed for public tours, and just one month and five days after it was found, it opened as a show cave. Since then, for more than 160 years, Diamond Caverns has been a local attraction. In the 1920s, there were 17 show caves in the area, one of which was Diamond Caverns. In order to compete with these other attractions, electric lights were installed, and the original wooden staircase was replaced with a concrete one to make visitation safer. Currently, cave tours are available year-round on a first-come, first-served basis.

Best Time to Visit: Diamond Caverns is open from 9:00 a.m. to 5:00 p.m. between March 20th and Labor Day. During the fall and winter, you need to call the attraction to schedule a tour.

Pass/Permit/Fees: Adult admission is $20, and children between the ages of four and 12 are $10.00.

Closest City or Town: Arthur, Kentucky

How to Get There: From Arthur, head southeast on KY-70 E and turn right onto KY-255. The Caverns are on the left at 1900 Mammoth Cave Pkwy.

GPS Coordinates: 37.11721° N, -86.06213° W

Did You Know? Diamond Caverns is the second-oldest show cave in Kentucky and the fourth oldest in the United States.

Mammoth Cave National Park

Known as the longest cave system in the world, Mammoth Cave National Park spans 52,830 acres and surrounds the Green River and the Big Clifty Sandstone. More than 400 miles of surveyed passageways make up the cave system in the park—which was specifically created to protect the caves. There are several tours of the cave that visitors can take, which will take them past the Grand Avenue, Fat Man's Misery, and Frozen Niagara features, along with many other formations. For more adventurous guests, there is a wild tour that leads them away from the developed cave portions to muddy and dusty undeveloped tunnels.

Best Time to Visit: The cave stays at a constant temperature all year, so it is fine to visit year-round. Be aware that cave tours end at 4:30 p.m. in the winter and 5:00 p.m. in the summer.

Pass/Permit/Fees: There is no fee to visit the park, but there are varying fees for cave tours.

Closest City or Town: Arthur, Kentucky

How to Get There: From Arthur, head southeast on KY-70 and in 6.8 miles, turn left onto Mammoth Cave Entrance Rd/Mammoth Cave Pkwy.

GPS Coordinates: 37.18903° N, -86.09980° W

Did You Know? Prior to the 1990s, visitors could take the Echo River Tour, which was a boat tour on the underground river, through the cave system.

Nolin Lake State Park

This 333-acre park and 5,795-acre lake opened in 1996 to provide recreational opportunities to the surrounding community. There are 32 campsites with RV hookups and 27 primitive campsites available in the park, all with access to a public beach, laundry facilities, a playground, and shower facilities. Fishing is popular at Nolin Lake, as there are plenty of crappie, catfish, bass, and walleye to be caught. Be sure to have a valid Kentucky fishing license before you drop your line in the water. A 9.2-mile hiking trail leads to a small seasonal waterfall and can be used by walkers, bikers, and other non-motorized vehicles. The public beach is open between Memorial Day and Labor Day and provides a great location for a refreshing swim in the lake.

Best Time to Visit: The best time to visit is in the summer.

Pass/Permit/Fees: There is no fee to visit Nolin Lake State Park unless you camp overnight. Contact the park directly at 270-286-4240 for rates and availability.

Closest City or Town: Arthur, Kentucky

How to Get There: From Arthur, take KY-259 N and turn right onto KY-728 in 7.3 miles. Turn left onto State Hwy 1827, and Nolin Lake is in three miles.

GPS Coordinates: 37.30358° N, -86.20801° W

Did You Know? Nolin Lake is calm and serene, which makes it a perfect location for paddle boarding and kayaking.

The Green River

This 384-mile tributary of the Ohio River is located in south-central Kentucky and provides numerous opportunities for water activities such as canoeing, kayaking, fishing, floating, and white-water rafting. Along miles 188 to 210, the river flows freely through Mammoth Cave National Park, which is the result of the 2017 dismantling of a dam that prevented its natural flow. The Green River is one of the longest in Kentucky and is certainly the most navigable. Anglers love the river for its diverse fish population, including walleye, muskie, and sauger. In fact, there are more than 150 species of fish in the river, along with over 70 species of mussels. After the Revolutionary War ended, many soldiers were paid in land rights, which resulted in the establishment of settlements along the Green River.

Best Time to Visit: The best time to visit is in the summer.

Pass/Permit/Fees: There is no fee to visit the Green River.

Closest City or Town: Arthur, Kentucky

How to Get There: From Arthur, take KY-70 E to I-65 N. Use exit 65 to turn left onto US-31W S/Main St. In 1.6 miles, turn right onto Old St. and then left onto River Rd. There is a park with river access at 103-109 River Rd.

GPS Coordinates: 37.2687° N, -85.8872° W

Did You Know? Although there is no longer an "e" on the end, the river is named for General Nathanael Greene, a prominent soldier in the American Revolutionary War.

Anglin Falls

A 1.7-mile, mostly uphill trail takes hikers from the trailhead to a 75-foot waterfall in the John B. Stephenson Memorial Forest State Preserve. The trail is not well-marked and can be challenging in spots, especially due to the uneven terrain, but it should be accessible to hikers of most abilities. The sides of the waterfall are steep and lead to rocky ridge lines, so climbing to the top of the falls is not recommended, especially after rain when the rocks will be slippery. Along the route to the waterfall, you'll pass over 450 species of plants native to Kentucky, including 32 different ferns. In the spring, the wildflowers are in bloom and will provide a scenic journey to the area.

Best Time to Visit: Spring is the best time to visit, as the waterfall is at its fullest and flowers are starting to bloom.

Pass/Permit/Fees: There is no fee to visit Anglin Falls.

Closest City or Town: Berea, Kentucky

How to Get There: From Berea, follow KY-21 E to reach US-421 S. Turn right onto State Hwy 1912 and then right again onto Arvil Branstetters Rd. Stay on Arvil Branstetters Rd. to reach Anglin Falls.

GPS Coordinates: 37.50239° N, -84.21698° W

Did You Know? The trail to Anglin Falls is considered one of the best-kept secrets for viewing wildflowers in Kentucky. In the spring, if you visit when the ground is wet, one or two days after the last big rain or snow, you may even see some secondary falls along the route.

Pinnacles of Berea

The Pinnacles of Berea offer some of the most unobstructed views of Kentucky and the surrounding area in all directions. There are several locations where hikers can stop to take in the spectacular view, including the Main Lookout, East Pinnacle, West Pinnacle, Eagles Nest, Buzzards Roost, and Devils Kitchen. The lookouts are spread about one mile apart, with some trails more difficult than others. The most popular viewing point is the Main Lookout, but rock climbers prefer the West Pinnacle for its more challenging terrain. Most hikes are rated as moderate, but the West Pinnacle is not meant for beginners. Dogs are allowed on the trails as long as they are leashed, but camping is not available.

Best Time to Visit: The spring and fall are the best times to visit to witness the colors changing with the seasons.

Pass/Permit/Fees: There is no fee to visit the Pinnacles.

Closest City or Town: Berea, Kentucky

How to Get There: In Berea, head northeast on Chestnut St. and take a right onto Prospect St. Continue onto KY-21 E/Big Hill Rd. and the pinnacles are on the left in two miles, at 2047 Big Hill Rd.

GPS Coordinates: 37.55447° N, -84.24077° W

Did You Know? *Outside Magazine* listed the Pinnacles of Berea as the best hike in Kentucky for 2019 for the incredible views and variety of trails, both in terms of skill level and length.

Aviation Heritage Park

This park honors the lives of regional aviation heroes by telling their stories through static aircraft displays. You can see a T-38 trainer that every Mercury, Gemini, and Apollo astronaut flew, a Cub that was flown by an African American woman who trained the Tuskegee airmen, and a UH-1 Huey helicopter that served with the Green Hornets of the 20th Special Operations Squadron of the U.S. Air Force. There are numerous other aircraft on display as well, each of them with a story to tell about the pilots that flew them during their military service. Not only can you see the aircraft, but you're encouraged to touch them as well, to allow yourself to imagine what it was like to fly each one.

Best Time to Visit: Aviation Heritage Park is open daily from 8:00 a.m. to dusk. Since it is entirely outdoors, the best time to visit is in the spring or fall when the temperatures are mild.

Pass/Permit/Fees: There is no fee to visit the park.

Closest City or Town: Bowling Green, Kentucky

How to Get There: From Bowling Green, head northeast on Russellville Rd. and turn right onto US-231 S. Take a right onto Smallhouse Rd. to reach 1825 Three Sprigs Rd.

GPS Coordinates: 36.91899° N, -86.43633° W

Did You Know? Aviation Heritage Park was founded by Brigadier General Dan Cherry after he discovered the actual F-4 Phantom Fighter plane that he flew in Vietnam when he won an aerial battle over a MiG 21.

14

Basil Griffin Park

At 111 acres, Basil Griffin Park offers a large area for a variety of activities right in the city of Bowling Green. There is a 33-acre lake that is accessible by a public boat ramp for fishing, floating, and feeding the ducks and geese that call the lake home. This is also the location of Aviation Heritage Park, which displays several military aircraft honoring Kentucky aviators. Additionally, you'll have access to three basketball courts, a disc golf course, five baseball fields, a football field, five multipurpose fields, a soccer field, a hockey rink, a horseshoe pit, six playgrounds, two tennis courts, four picnic shelters, and much more. This is truly a community park that has a little something available for everyone.

Best Time to Visit: Basil Griffin Park is open daily from 8:00 a.m. to dusk. Since it's an outdoor facility, the best time to visit is spring, summer, or fall.

Pass/Permit/Fees: There is no fee to visit the park.

Closest City or Town: Bowling Green, Kentucky

How to Get There: In Bowling Green, head northeast on Russellville Rd. and turn right onto US-231 S. Turn right onto Smallhouse Rd. and then right onto Parkside Ln. to reach the park on the left at Three Springs Rd.

GPS Coordinates: 36.92003° N, -86.43913° W

Did You Know? Fishermen love Basil Griffin Park for its abundant stock of white crappie, largemouth bass, redear sunfish, carp, bluegill, channel catfish, and rainbow trout.

Beech Bend Park

Beech Bend Park is an amusement park, raceway, and campground that provides hours of fun for visitors of all ages. Rides such as the Kentucky Rumbler, Moby Dick, Sea Dragon, Vortex, Zero-G, and many more will satisfy your need for adventure. The raceway is a drag strip that showcases some of the fastest cars in the region. The campground has more than 400 camping sites, with more than half offering full RV hookups.

Best Time to Visit: The amusement park is open from 10:30, 11:00 a.m., or 12:30 p.m. to 6:00 p.m., 6:30 p.m., 7:00 p.m., 8:00 p.m., or 9:00 p.m. depending on the day you visit. View the website for the raceway's most current events calendar.

Pass/Permit/Fees: Adults 48 inches tall or taller are $37.99, and children under 48 inches tall are $31.99. Children under the age of two are free.

Closest City or Town: Bowling Green, Kentucky

How to Get There: In Bowling Green, head northeast on Russellville Rd. and turn left onto US-68 E/Veterans Memorial Ln. Turn left onto Victoria St., which will turn slightly right to become Double Springs Rd. Turn left onto Beech Bend Rd. and right onto Beech Bend Park Rd. Stay right to reach 798 Beech Bend Park Rd.

GPS Coordinates: 37.02247° N, -86.40153° W

Did You Know? There has been an amusement park at the Beech Bend Park location since 1898.

Bowling Green Hot Rods

The Bowling Green Hot Rods is a minor league baseball team that is a High-A affiliate of the Major League Baseball team, the Tampa Bay Rays. The team plays its home games at Bowling Green Ballpark, which opened in 2009. The stadium has a capacity of 4,559 seats and ten luxury suites. It also features a 35-foot-by-56-foot video board, a splash pad, and a 6-foot-by-3-foot-by-68-foot LED ribbon board around the stadium. There are a variety of promotions that make the game fun, including "Get Out Me Swamp Night," "Wizard Night," and "Peace, Love, and Hotrods Night," among many others.

Best Time to Visit: The best time to visit the Bowling Green Hot Rods is during baseball season, which runs from late March to the end of September.

Pass/Permit/Fees: The cost varies based on game and seat selection.

Closest City or Town: Bowling Green, Kentucky

How to Get There: In Bowling Green, head northeast on Russellville Rd. and turn left onto University Blvd., which turns right and becomes Kentucky St. Turn right onto E 8th Ave to reach 300 E 8th Ave.

GPS Coordinates: 36.99733° N, -86.44142° W

Did You Know? The Bowling Green Hot Rods got their name from the city's connections to the automobile industry.

Capitol Arts Center/SKyPAC

The Capitol Arts Center is a performing arts complex now known as SKyPAC that hosts concerts, touring performances, and various community events. What began as a vaudeville house in the late 19th century first evolved into the Columbia Theatre in the 1930s and then into the Capitol Arts Center in 1981. At one point, in 1967, the center theatre closed and was vacant for over a decade before the Bowling Green-Warren County Arts Commission purchased the building to complete a $1.3 million renovation into the center that's known today. A more recent $6.7 million renovation in 2000 turned the Capitol Arts Center into a much larger facility called the Southern Kentucky Performing Arts Center, or SKyPAC.

Best Time to Visit: The best time to visit the Capitol Arts Center/SKyPAC is when there is a show you want to see playing at the center. Shows are listed on their website.

Pass/Permit/Fees: The fee to visit the Capitol Arts Center/SKyPAC depends on your show and seat selection.

Closest City or Town: Bowling Green, Kentucky

How to Get There: In Bowling Green, the Capitol Arts Center is located off of E Main Ave. at 416 E Main Ave.

GPS Coordinates: 36.99432° N, -86.44120° W

Did You Know? The art galleries at the Capitol Arts Center/SKyPAC, which hosts various art exhibitions throughout the year, can be visited for free on Monday through Friday from 10:00 a.m. to 5:00 p.m.

Fountain Square Park

This Civil War-era park was conceived in 1870 and features gorgeous seasonal landscaping that is spectacular in the spring, summer, and fall. Fountain Square has been the site of prohibitionists, trolleys, parades, and even scrap drives. It used to be the location of animal auctions, pageants, and swap meets, but today, it's an ideal place for a relaxing day in nature. When the park was first created, the focal point was a two-tiered limestone fountain and reflection pool, but by 1881, the fountain was in complete disrepair and required replacement. The statues around the fountain were meant to represent the four seasons: Ceres (goddess of grain), Pomona (goddess of fruit), Melpomene (goddess of tragedy), and Flora (goddess of flowers).

Best Time to Visit: The best time to visit Fountain Square Park is spring, summer, or fall to see seasonal vegetation.

Pass/Permit/Fees: There is no fee to visit the park.

Closest City or Town: Bowling Green, Kentucky

How to Get There: In Bowling Green, follow Russellville Rd., turn right onto University Blvd., left onto Normal St., and then continue onto State St. Keep left to stay on State St., and then take a slight left onto E Main Ave., and the park is at 445 E Main Ave.

GPS Coordinates: 36.99403° N, -86.44148° W

Did You Know? The Bowling Green Garden Club of 1934 was initially responsible for developing and tending the lush vegetation of Fountain Square Park.

Historic Railpark and Train Museum

Bowling Green, Kentucky has an extensive history with transportation in the state, from steamboats to the railroad, to the highway system. The L&N Depot, which is now the Historic Railpark and Train Museum, was constructed in 1925. At its peak, there were more than 20 trains departing from the L&N Depot each day, which fueled Bowling Green's economy via hundreds of travelers passing through the city. On the 450-foot track behind the museum, you'll discover an E8 Engine, the Duncan Hines Diner Car, a Railroad Post Office Car, the 353 Presidential Office Car, a 1953 Pullman Sleeper, and a Chessie Class C027 Caboose.

Best Time to Visit: The museum is open late May to October 31, Sunday through Saturday, from 10:00 a.m. to 4:00 p.m.

Pass/Permit/Fees: Adult admission is $16 per person, children ages five to 12 are $10, and seniors ages 60 and over are $14. Children ages four and under are free.

Closest City or Town: Bowling Green, Kentucky

How to Get There: In Bowling Green, head northeast on Russellville Rd. for 1.5 miles. Turn left onto University Blvd., which will turn right and become Kentucky St. Take a left onto Depot Ave. to reach 401 Kentucky St.

GPS Coordinates: 37.00093° N, -86.43807° W

Did You Know? The museum offers various interactive displays telling the story of the regional and national importance of the railroad.

Lost River Cave

This historic cave is a wonderful example of the limestone caves in the state. Take an underground boat through the cave, or hike along the various above-ground trails that will take you past scenic outcrops, sinking streams, and blue holes. You can also visit a seasonal butterfly habitat, a paved greenway trail, and a man-made wetland system. The cave and 25-acre wooded surroundings were donated to Western Kentucky University by professor Dr. Raymond Cravens, Owen Larson, and Mr. and Mrs. Leroy Highbaugh in 1986. It wasn't until 1999 that the cave was opened to float tours, but since then, the Lost River Cave has provided thousands of visitors with educational information about the geology of the area and the formation of caves.

Best Time to Visit: Cave tours run from 8:30 a.m. to 6:30 p.m., Monday through Sunday, except on major holidays.

Pass/Permit/Fees: Adult admission is $21.95 on Monday through Thursday and $22.95 on Friday through Sunday. Youth ages four through 12 are $16.95, and children three and under are $5.95 on all days.

Closest City or Town: Bowling Green, Kentucky

How to Get There: From Bowling Green, head northeast on Russellville Rd. and then take a right onto US-231 S. Turn right onto Nashville Rd. to reach the Lost River Cave.

GPS Coordinates: 36.95379° N, -86.47334° W

Did You Know? The Flying Squirrel Zipline is also an attraction available here for $34.95 for an hour tour.

National Corvette Museum

Sports car fans will love the National Corvette Museum, an attraction that celebrates the Chevrolet Corvette, a vehicle that has been assembled in Kentucky since 1981. The exterior of the museum is well-known for its innovative architecture, which was inspired by the Corvette itself. The 115,000-square-foot building represents a complete departure from the traditional rectangular museum and features curved walls, full-scale diorama exhibits, and geometric design to celebrate the history of the Corvette. You'll see over 80 Corvettes from all periods since 1953, but because the museum rotates its displays, you'll never see the same exact cars, even if you visit multiple times.

Best Time to Visit: The museum is open daily from 8:00 a.m. to 5:00 p.m.

Pass/Permit/Fees: Adult admission is $15 per person, children between the ages of five and 12 are $10, and seniors ages 62 and older are $13. Children ages four and under are free.

Closest City or Town: Bowling Green, Kentucky

How to Get There: From Bowling Green, use Old Porter Pike to reach Porter Pike. Turn left onto Corvette Dr. The museum is on the left at 350 Corvette Dr.

GPS Coordinates: 37.00479° N, -86.37471° W

Did You Know? Other fun exhibits include interactive quizzes, photographic opportunities, and the 200-seat Chevrolet Theater.

General Burnside Island State Park

This unique state park is located on an island in the middle of Lake Cumberland. It includes an award-winning 18-hole regulation public golf course, a marina, campsites, hiking trails, and abundant fishing opportunities. Anglers flock to this park and drop their line in Lake Cumberland to catch their fill of crappie, largemouth bass, smallmouth bass, and striped bass. Fishing is allowed, and equipment can be rented from the full-service marina. Fishing boats, ski boats, houseboats, and pontoon boats are all available to rent. There are 94 campsites on the island available between mid-March and mid-November, all with utility hookups.

Best Time to Visit: Summer is the best time to visit General Burnside Island State Park to take advantage of the water activities.

Pass/Permit/Fees: There is no fee to visit the park, but individual activities like golf will require a fee.

Closest City or Town: Burnside, Kentucky

How to Get There: In Burnside, head southeast on US-27 S. Turn right onto Ic-1001, and then left onto Ic-1005. The park is on the right at 8801 US-27.

GPS Coordinates: 36.97410° N, -84.60364° W

Did You Know? The park is named in honor of the Civil War Union General Ambrose Burnside, who was known for his sideburn whiskers.

Lake Barkley

As the second lake mentioned in the name "Land Between the Lakes Recreation Area," Lake Barkley is slightly smaller than its older sibling, Kentucky Lake, but it still provides numerous recreational opportunities, including fishing, boating, and swimming. Even though Kentucky Lake has more square feet of water, Lake Barkley holds more water because it's deeper, which means there are additional fish species to be found in Lake Barkley beyond what you'll find at Kentucky Lake. Bass and crappie fishing are the best you'll find in the state, but there are also plenty of bluegills, several species of catfish, sauger, shell crackers, crappie, redear, and yellow perch just waiting for your hook. If you don't have your own boat or fishing gear, you can rent both at the full-service marina.

Best Time to Visit: Spring and fall are best for fishing, and summer is ideal for swimming.

Pass/Permit/Fees: There is no fee to visit Lake Barkley.

Closest City or Town: Cadiz, Kentucky

How to Get There: From Cadiz, follow US-68 W for nine miles, and then turn left onto Forest Service Rd. 159-N. On the right, you'll find Devil's Elbow Day Use Area, which provides access to the lake.

GPS Coordinates: 36.8172° N, -87.9988° W

Did You Know? Lake Barkley is home to the largest yellow bass to ever be caught in Kentucky (1 pound, 1 ounce).

24

Indian Staircase Trail

The Indian Staircase Trail, located in the Red River Gorge, is a difficult hike that will take you to the Indian Arch, the KY 80 Arch, and various other geological wonders in the gorge. West of the ridge line at the top of the Indian Staircase, you can explore the largest rock shelter in the gorge. It is over 100 yards in length, and if you hike through the shelter, it will take you back to the main trail around the ridge. The trail is full of rocky spots that will require scrambles, which is why it is not recommended for beginning hikers or for those with physical challenges. Additionally, the trail is not well-marked, so you'll want to pay careful attention to the red arrows on the trees.

Best Time to Visit: Spring and fall are the best times to visit for the wildflowers and the changing leaves.

Pass/Permit/Fees: There is a $3 per vehicle per day fee to enter the Daniel Boone National Forest to access the trail.

Closest City or Town: Campton, Kentucky

How to Get There: From Campton, take Mountain Parkway Spur to merge onto Bert T Combs Mountain Pkwy W. Take exit 40 toward Pine Ridge, and then left onto KY-15 N. Turn right and stay on KY-715 N until you reach the trail at 3451 Sky Bridge Rd.

GPS Coordinates: 37.84789° N, -83.61613° W

Did You Know? If you prefer a less strenuous hike to the top of the Indian Staircase Trail, hike it counterclockwise to climb instead of descending the staircase.

Natural Bridge State Resort Park

The Natural Bridge State Resort Park wasn't officially a park until 1926, but it attracted tourists all the way back to 1895 when the Lexington and Eastern Railroad passed over the 30-foot-wide natural sandstone arch. Located in the Daniel Boone National Forest, the Natural Bridge State Resort Park encompasses 2,300 acres and features the 78-foot-long, 65-feet-high natural bridge. In addition to crossing the natural bridge, there are also more than 20 miles of hiking trails taking guests to White's Branch Arch and other points of interest throughout the park. If you decide not to hike to the top of the arch, you can take the 11-minute Sky Lift to the top instead.

Best Time to Visit: Spring and fall are the best times to visit the Natural Bridge State Resort Park.

Pass/Permit/Fees: There is a $3 per day, per vehicle fee to visit the Daniel Boone National Park. There is no additional fee to visit the Natural Bridge State Resort Park.

Closest City or Town: Campton, Kentucky

How to Get There: From Campton, take Bert T Combs Mountain Pkwy. W to exit 33 for KY-11 toward Slade/Beattyville. Follow KY-11 S for 2.1 miles to reach the park at 2135 Natural Bridge Rd.

GPS Coordinates: 37.77560° N, -83.68662° W

Did You Know? The Kentucky Reptile Zoo is located in the park and is open for tours to see how researchers are extracting venom for antivenom and biomedical research.

Red River Gorge

Located in east-central Kentucky, the Red River Gorge passes through the Daniel Boone National Forest and features over 100 natural sandstone arches, a multitude of sandstone cliffs, and the 900-foot-long Nada Tunnel, which is a man-made logging tunnel blasted out between 1910 and 1912 to provide a more convenient way through the gorge. Throughout the gorge, numerous Native American artifacts have been found, some dating back to the Paleoindian Period. The gorge is a popular place for rock climbers due to the towering cliffs in the area. Climbers from across the globe come to the Red River Gorge to climb "Big Red."

Best Time to Visit: The best time to visit the Red River Gorge is during the spring or fall to avoid the heat of the summer.

Pass/Permit/Fees: There is a $3 per vehicle, per day fee to enter the Daniel Boone National Forest to access the gorge.

Closest City or Town: Campton, Kentucky

How to Get There: From Campton, take Bert T Combs Mountain Pkwy. W to exit 40. Turn left onto KY-15 N, and then right onto KY-715 N. Red River Gorge is in 6.3 miles.

GPS Coordinates: 37.82704° N, -83.56728° W

Did You Know? The Sky Bridge, one of the sandstone bridges in the Red River Gorge, was the setting for part of the 1955 film "The Kentuckian," which starred Burt Lancaster.

Crystal Onyx Cave

Discovered in 1960 by Cleon Turner, the Crystal Onyx Cave opened as a commercial show cave in 1965. The cave features a one-hour tour that allows visitors to get up close and personal with a variety of cave formations, a sinkhole, and more in this living natural structure. Additionally, since the cave's reopening in 2018, the stairs, bridge, railings, and trails have all been replaced or renovated to improve guests' experience. New LED lighting also helps visitors to better see the incredible formations inside the cave. Several new openings have been discovered since the original passages were found in 1960.

Best Time to Visit: Cave tours are available every day between March 1 and October 31 from 10:00 a.m. to 6:00 p.m.

Pass/Permit/Fees: Adult admission is $16, and children between the ages of four and 12 are $13. Children ages three and under are free.

Closest City or Town: Cave City, Kentucky

How to Get There: From Cave City, use US-31 W S to reach KY-90 E/E Happy Valley St. Turn right at Caveland Rd. and continue straight onto Prewitts Knob Rd. until you reach the Crystal Onyx Cave at 425 Prewitts Knob Rd.

GPS Coordinates: 37.11153° N, -85.97466° W

Did You Know? Several full human skeletons were found in the cave that was determined to be 2,600 years old. The cave was likely a former burial ground.

Dog Slaughter Falls

Dog Slaughter Falls is a waterfall located in the London Ranger District of the Daniel Boone National Forest. The 2.4-mile trail that leads to the 15-foot falls is surrounded by picturesque stands of hemlock trees and rhododendron bushes. You'll also pass by massive boulders, some of which appear to be perched in precarious positions. You can actually reach the falls by two separate trails: the Dog Slaughter Trail, which is an upstream hike, or the Sheltowee Trace Trail, which is a downstream hike. Both trails are rated moderately easy and are accessible to hikers of all abilities.

Best Time to Visit: Since the river runs fastest and fullest during the spring when rainstorms are frequent, and the snow melt increases the volume, the best time to visit Dog Slaughter Falls is during the spring.

Pass/Permit/Fees: There is a $3 per vehicle, per day fee to visit the Daniel Boone National Forest to access the falls.

Closest City or Town: Corbin, Kentucky

How to Get There: From Corbin, take Hwy 727 to US-25W S. In 3.8 miles, turn right onto Devils Creek Rd. and continue onto Daniel Boone Forest Rd. to reach the falls.

GPS Coordinates: 36.86060° N, -84.31098° W

Did You Know? Rumor has it that Dog Slaughter Falls got its name either from people using the river to drown unwanted pets or from the loss of hunting dogs in the forest due to the abundance of predatory wildlife.

Eagle Falls Trail

Located in Cumberland Falls State Resort Park, the Eagle Falls Trail is a 1.5-mile journey from the trailhead to the falls. It can be challenging in the spring because the lower section can be under water during the spring, and because the last section of the trail is characterized by rough terrain. The 44-foot vertical plunge in Eagle Falls is one of the best-kept secrets in the state. After a nice rain, this waterfall rivals the beauty of any other waterfall in Kentucky. Even if the falls aren't running strong, you will still enjoy the area behind the falls, in the small rock shelter carved into the cliffside.

Best Time to Visit: The best time to visit is during the spring when the falls will be running full and fast.

Pass/Permit/Fees: There is no fee to visit Eagle Falls Trail.

Closest City or Town: Corbin, Kentucky

How to Get There: From Corbin, follow N Kentucky Ave. to W 4th St. In 0.8 miles, continue onto State Hwy 727/W 5th Street Rd. Turn right onto US-25 W S, and in 3.8 miles, turn right onto US-25 W S. In 6.1 miles, take a slight right onto KY-90 W and continue until you reach the falls.

GPS Coordinates: 36.84655° N, -84.34321° W

Did You Know? On the way to Eagle Falls, there are several outcroppings that will allow you to get different views of Cumberland Falls, but they can be obscured by foliage in the spring and summer.

Harland Sanders Café and Museum

The Harland Sanders Café is the first restaurant opened by the man who would one day become the Colonel Sanders of Kentucky Fried Chicken fame. The café is preserved in the style of the 1940s and 1950s when the restaurant operated the eatery. The famous KFC secret recipe that would become synonymous with fried chicken in the U.S. was developed at this restaurant. You'll learn about Harland Sanders and his numerous business ventures, including a service station in Corbin before he opened his restaurant. Along with discovering more about Sanders, you'll also discover his innovative open kitchen and model motel room that was added to the café to entice travelers to stay in Sanders' next-door motel.

Best Time to Visit: The museum is open Monday through Sunday from 10:00 a.m. to 10:00 p.m.

Pass/Permit/Fees: There is no fee to visit the Harland, only to order Kentucky Fried Chicken from its source.

Closest City or Town: Corbin, Kentucky

How to Get There: In Corbin, head north on N Main St. and continue onto US-25W N. Turn left to stay on US-25 W N, and the destination is on the left at 688 US-25W.

GPS Coordinates: 36.96072° N, -84.09369° W

Did You Know? In 1939, the original Harland Café was destroyed by fire. Sanders didn't give up; he rebuilt the current structure along with a motel next door, both of which opened on July 4, 1940.

Rockcastle River

Forming the border between Rockcastle County and Laurel County, the Rockcastle River is a popular location for whitewater rafting. There is a floatable section of the river that begins where the Middle Fork and South Fork of Rockcastle River converge, and because it is so calm, it's a perfect place for fishermen, beginning rafters, and canoers. The middle section of Rockcastle River is more challenging but still a great place for novice rafters and experienced canoeists and kayakers who can recover after significant drops. The area after Old Howard Place Access, though, features near-Class III rapids, and only highly experienced rafters and boaters with superior technical skills should attempt this part of the river.

Best Time to Visit: Summer is ideal for swimming.

Pass/Permit/Fees: There is a $3 per vehicle, per day fee to enter Daniel Boone National Forest to access the river.

Closest City or Town: Corbin, Kentucky

How to Get There: From Corbin, follow KY-312 W for 8.3 miles, and then turn left onto KY-192 W. In 6.5 miles, take a slight left onto KY-1193 S, and then continue straight onto KY-3497 to reach Rockcastle River.

GPS Coordinates: 37.22756° N, -84.26214° W

Did You Know? Rockcastle River was discovered by Dr. Thomas Walker in 1750 and was originally named the Lawless River because of its powerful rapids.

Great American Dollhouse Museum

The Great American Dollhouse Museum provides a glimpse of U.S. history through the dollhouses it has on display. You'll start with a Native American dollhouse, then pass through history by viewing one from the Colonial, Old West, Southwest, and Victorian eras. Your trip through U.S. history will end with a modern dollhouse, complete with a hot tub and cell phones. There are other dollhouse exhibits as well, including one of Copper Hollow around 1910 that depicts its neighborhoods, streets, and open land in a continuous exhibit. These historically accurate displays are an innovative way to teach American history and how the lives of everyday people were lived.

Best Time to Visit: The museum is open Wednesday through Saturday from 11:00 a.m. to 5:00 p.m.

Pass/Permit/Fees: Adult admission is $12, and children between the ages of four and 16 are $8. Seniors are $10, and children under the age of four are free.

Closest City or Town: Danville, Kentucky

How to Get There: In Danville, head onto W Main St., turn right onto N 5th St., and then left onto W Lexington Ave. Turn right onto Swope Dr., and the museum is on the right at 344 Swope Dr.

GPS Coordinates: 37.65083° N, -84.77837° W

Did You Know? The interactive Dollhouse Village allows children to play with furnished dollhouses, a miniature shopping mall, and horse stables.

Pennyrile Forest State Resort Park

Pennyrile Forest State Resort Park is named for the Pennyroyal plant that is prevalent throughout the woodlands around the park. There is a 56-acre lake (Lake Beshear) that provides visitors with the opportunity to take a pedal boat, canoe, kayak, rowboat, or a standup paddleboard out on the water. Fishermen will find plenty of channel catfish, largemouth bass, crappie, or bluegill in the lake with a valid Kentucky fishing license. An 18-hole golf course, basketball courts, tennis courts, hiking, horseback riding, and miniature golf provide guests with numerous onshore activities throughout the park. Birdwatching is also popular, with sightings of nuthatches, purple finches, cedar waxwings, Carolina chickadees, warblers, rose-breasted grosbeaks, and yellow-billed cuckoos.

Best Time to Visit: Spring and fall are ideal for birdwatching and fishing.

Pass/Permit/Fees: There is no fee to enter the park, but there are varying fees for activities.

Closest City or Town: Dawson Springs, Kentucky

How to Get There: From Dawson Springs, use KY-109 S/Scott St. to reach Dawson Springs Rd/Old Kentucky 398 in 5.5 miles. In half a mile, turn right onto KY-398 S, and the park is in 2.6 miles.

GPS Coordinates: 37.07322° N, -87.66295° W

Did You Know? Be sure to hike to Fisherman's Rock for spectacular views of the park.

34

Breaks Interstate Park

Located at the border of Kentucky and Virginia, Breaks Interstate Park is full of outdoor activities to enjoy, from rafting, climbing, and camping, to birdwatching, hiking, and fishing. The Russell Fork River runs through an immense, awe-inspiring gorge that is thought to be the largest gorge east of the Mississippi River. The botany in the area is diverse, as 180 million years ago, a massive inland sea receded and left fractal ferns, coltsfoot, galax, tea berries, and various fungi and moss species behind. The colors of this flora mélange provide a magnificent backdrop for photos. Fishing is available in Laurel Lake and the Russell Fork River, with plenty of rainbow trout, bluegill, and bass.

Best Time to Visit: For hiking, climbing, fishing, and birdwatching, spring and fall are the best times to visit.

Pass/Permit/Fees: There is no fee to visit Breaks Interstate Park, but there are fees required for individual activities such as swimming and golf. Contact the park directly at 276-865-4413 for these rates.

Closest City or Town: Elkhorn City, Kentucky

How to Get There: From Elkhorn, head southeast on KY-80 E, and continue until you can take a right onto State Rt. 702 to reach Breaks Interstate Park at 627 Commission Cir.

GPS Coordinates: 37.29739° N, -82.31748° W

Did You Know? Much of this park is actually in Virginia, but you can access it from either state.

Kentucky State Capitol

Constructed between 1904 and 1910, the current Kentucky State Capitol is the fourth building to serve as the capitol since Kentucky became a state in 1792. There had been a long battle about where to build the capitol. This fight ended in 1904 when the state legislature voted to appropriate $1 million to build a new building to replace the 1830 capitol building in downtown Frankfort. The design for the new capitol proved to be much larger than the previous structure, so it was moved to a bigger area in south Frankfort. The architect on the project was Frank Mills Andrews, who favored the Beaux-Arts architectural style, so many of the opulent decorative features of the Capitol are reminiscent of Andrews's love of classical French interiors.

Best Time to Visit: Tours are available Monday through Friday from 8:00 a.m. to 4:30 p.m., and the best time to visit would be during a legislative session.

Pass/Permit/Fees: There is no fee to visit the capitol.

Closest City or Town: Frankfort, Kentucky

How to Get There: In Frankfort, head onto W Main St. and then turn right onto Capital Ave./War Mothers Memorial Bridge. Stay on Capital Ave. to the capitol.

GPS Coordinates: 38.18756° N, -84.87537° W

Did You Know? The Capitol design did not include considerations for parking, as the automobile was viewed as a fad that would pass.

Locust Grove

Locust Grove is a mansion built in 1792 by William and Lucy Clark Croghan. The mansion was built, and the land was later worked by slaves until the Croghan family sold the property to riverboat captain James Paul in 1878. In 1883, the mansion and land were again sold, this time to Richard Waters of Heritage Farm. The state of Kentucky and Jefferson County purchased the house and 55 acres of land in 1961 with the intent to restore and preserve the original structure.

Best Time to Visit: Locust Grove is open Tuesday through Saturday from 10:00 a.m. to 4:30 p.m. Various tours are available throughout the week. The museum is closed in January and February.

Pass/Permit/Fees: Adult admission is $12 per person, and children between the ages of six and 18 are $6 per person. Seniors are $10 per person.

Closest City or Town: Frankfort, Kentucky

How to Get There: From Frankfort, take I-75 north for 50.8 miles to Paris Street in Williamstown. Then follow W State Highway 22 to Gumlick Road in Pendleton County, where the mansion is located.

GPS Coordinates: 38.64037° N, -84.48800° W

Did You Know? At one point, Locust Grove was the site of a duel between Kentucky statesman Cassius Marcellus Clay and Robert Wickliffe, Jr. There was no conclusive winner of this fight.

Rebecca Ruth Candy Store & Museum

Rebecca Ruth's candy has been a Frankfort institution since its very first Bourbon Balls hit the shelves in 1919. Now, over 100 years later, visitors flock to the store and museum to sample the candy maker's Bourbon caramels, peanut brittle, chocolate-covered cherries, vanilla cremes, Kentucky Irish coffee bonbons, pecan-topped chocolate Bourbon balls, and pulled cream candy. Rebecca Ruth is known as the "Mother of Bourbon Balls," and you'll learn even more about her incredible life on your tour of the candy store and museum. The candy store is now owned by the fourth generation of Ruths, who continue to use the same recipes and techniques used more than a century ago.

Best Time to Visit: Tours of the candy store and museum are available Monday through Saturday from 10:30 a.m. to 2:30 p.m., and the store is open from 10:00 a.m. to 6:00 p.m. Monday through Sunday.

Pass/Permit/Fees: Adult admission is $6 per person, and children ages zero to 17 are $4 per person.

Closest City or Town: Frankfort, Kentucky

How to Get There: In Frankfort, continue on W Main St. and turn right onto Capital Ave. Take a left onto E 2nd St. and the museum is on the left at 116 E 2nd St.

GPS Coordinates: 38.19567° N, -84.87347° W

Did You Know? Candy production at the store only occurs Monday through Thursday, so if you want a tour of this aspect of the store, choose these days to visit.

Salato Wildlife Center

The Salato Wildlife Center is a 262-acre must-see destination for outdoor enthusiasts. There are indoor exhibits that include the Living Bee Tree, a Warm Water Aquarium, Snakes of Kentucky, and Alligator Snapping Turtle; outdoor exhibits that include Bison, Bald Eagles, Turkey, Bobcats, Elk, Deer, the Dragonfly Marsh, a Monarch Waystation, four miles of hiking trails, and more. While the center is often filled with students on field trips, you can visit it on your own and enjoy the exhibits that will teach you all you need to know about Kentucky wildlife.

Best Time to Visit: The center is open mid-March through November 24th, Tuesday through Saturday from 9:00 a.m. to 4:00 p.m.

Pass/Permit/Fees: Adult admission is $5 per person, and youths ages five through 18 are $3. Children ages four and under are free.

Closest City or Town: Frankfort, Kentucky

How to Get There: In Frankfort, head northeast on Elk Alley and turn left onto Mero St. Continue onto US-127 S. In 2.8 miles, turn right onto US-60 W, and then take another right onto KY-2270. In half a mile, turn left to reach the wildlife center at 1 Sportsman's Ln.

GPS Coordinates: 38.17846° N, -84.92329° W

Did You Know? The Salato Wildlife Center is named for Dr. James C. Salato, who was a Kentucky Fish and Wildlife Resources Commissioner for 28 years.

Old Friends Farm

Established in 2003, Old Friends Farm is a facility that takes in rescued horses, those retired from racing, or horses surrendered by their owners. On the 236-acre farm, there are more than 200 horses that are enjoying the twilight of their lives as approximately 20,000 visitors come to see these incredible animals each year. For example, Breeders' Cup Champions Little Mike, Amazombie, and Alphabet Soup live at the farm, along with Belmont Stakes winners Touch Gold and Sarava. These are just the high-profile horses that support the many other animals who struggled as racehorses but still need a place to live after their careers have ended.

Best Time to Visit: The farms are open Thursday through Sunday from 10:00 a.m. to 2:00 p.m., but tour reservations are required. See the website for booking details.

Pass/Permit/Fees: Tours are between $15 and $75 per person, depending on the chosen tour.

Closest City or Town: Georgetown, Kentucky

How to Get There: In Georgetown, use E Main St. to turn left onto Paynes Depot Rd. Take a right onto Neel Ln., a left, and the farm is on the right at 1841 Paynes Depot Rd.

GPS Coordinates: 38.18012° N, -84.59584° W

Did You Know? Old Friends Farm received a Special Eclipse Award in 2014 in recognition of its service in the sport of Thoroughbred racing.

Land Between the Lakes

The Land Between the Lakes has been a National Recreation Area since 1963. Located between Kentucky Lake and Barkley Lake, it offers visitors numerous recreational opportunities in one of the largest sections of undeveloped forest in the eastern portion of the U.S. There are 300 miles of natural shoreline, campsites, picnic areas, hiking trails, and fishing holes to enjoy. There are over 500 miles of trails available for hiking and biking, horseback riding, and ATV riding, and there's even a year-round horse camp available for equestrians. You can either take a self-guided tour of the area or request a guided tour from a professional naturalist who will take you through the Elk & Bison Prairie, the Woodlands Nature Station, the Golden Pond Planetarium, and the Homeplace 1850s Working Farm and Living History Museum.

Best Time to Visit: For water sports enthusiasts, the best time to visit the Land Between the Lakes is summer.

Pass/Permit/Fees: There is no fee to visit, but there are various rates for individual activities.

Closest City or Town: Golden Pond, Kentucky

How to Get There: From Golden Pond, take US-68 W to US-68 E to reach the recreation area at 238 Visitor Center Dr. in just over eight miles.

GPS Coordinates: 36.77782° N, -88.06343° W

Did You Know? More than 1.5 million people visit the Land Between the Lakes each year.

Kentucky Route 453 S

Kentucky Route 453 S is a 16-mile scenic highway that begins in Smithland in Livingston County and ends at the bridge that connects Kentucky Lake and Lake Barkley, just south of the Lyon County line. This road passes through the Land Between the Lakes Recreation Area, which makes it one of the prettiest drives in the state. Grand Rivers, which is the village situated between the two lakes, offers a variety of activities and lodging options for travelers. While you're there, take a look at the former home of Boston financier Thomas Lawson when he was attempting to promote Grand Rivers as the next great steel-making city, and the downtown area that has a bit of an old-west feel with its general store and upper-level balconies.

Best Time to Visit: The best time to drive is during the fall.

Pass/Permit/Fees: There is no fee to travel this route.

Closest City or Town: Grand Rivers, Kentucky

How to Get There: From Grand Rivers, head west on Ohio Ave. and turn left onto JH O'Bryan Ave. Take a right onto W Mississippi Ave. and a left onto Dover Rd. to reach KY-453 S.

GPS Coordinates: 37.13696° N, -88.39887° W

Did You Know? Kentucky Route 453 S is the perfect drive through eastern Kentucky for seeing the incredible fall foliage. It is lined with various tree species that produce leaves in stunning reds, oranges, and yellows.

Kentucky Lake

In terms of surface area, Kentucky Lake is the largest man-made lake east of the Mississippi River and boasts 2,064 miles of shoreline. Along with Lake Barkley, Kentucky Lake is one of the two lakes referenced in the name "Land Between the Lakes National Recreation Area." Two state parks, Kenlake State Resort Park in the west and Kentucky Dam Village State Resort Park in the north, use Kentucky Lake as their main recreational attraction. Fishermen come to the lake to catch some of the abundant bluegill, largemouth bass, yellow bass, and redear sunfish in the water. In fact, the lake holds state records for producing the largest buffalo carp (55 pounds), yellow perch (1 pound, 4 ounces), and white bass (5 pounds) in Kentucky.

Best Time to Visit: The best time to visit Kentucky Lake is in the summer, especially to participate in water sports.

Pass/Permit/Fees: There is no fee to visit Kentucky Lake.

Closest City or Town: Hamlin, Kentucky

How to Get There: In Hamlin, from State Hwy 444, turn left onto Blood River Rd. In 2.4 miles, take a left onto Bailey Cemetery Rd. and a left onto Oakshores Dr. to reach the lake.

GPS Coordinates: 36.61904° N, -88.04473° W

Did You Know? Kentucky Lake is the largest body of water between the Gulf of Mexico and the Great Lakes. It is the 25th largest lake overall and the 7th largest man-made lake in the U.S.

Cherokee State Park

Cherokee State Park is no longer a separate park with a separate entrance; instead, it's a part of Kenlake State Resort Park. However, it is still commemorated for its unique historical role. The park opened in 1951 as the only segregated state park in the southern part of the United States. Designated as a blacks-only state park, Cherokee State Park was approximately 300 acres in size and featured a 200-seat dining hall, fishing docks, a boat ramp, a bathhouse, a restaurant, and 12 cottages. In the 1950s, the park was considered the best park for a vacation for southern African Americans and attracted visitors from nearby states. The park closed when desegregation laws passed, and the cottages were relocated to Kenlake Park. The dining hall still stands today and has undergone several renovations.

Best Time to Visit: The best time to visit is in the summer.

Pass/Permit/Fees: There is no fee to visit Cherokee State Park.

Closest City or Town: Hardin, Kentucky

How to Get There: From Hardin, take KY-402 to US-68. Turn right onto KY-80 W, and then turn left onto Kenlake Rd. to reach the park.

GPS Coordinates: 37.19826 N, -88.19698° W

Did You Know? Under the "separate but equal" doctrine, Cherokee State Park was the only segregated state park in Kentucky.

Shaker Village of Pleasant Hill

Between 1805 and 1910, this area of Kentucky was home to the third-largest Shaker community in the country. Shaker Village of Pleasant Hill serves as a preserved Shaker community to allow visitors to explore and participate in various daily activities from the 19th and early 20th centuries. The Historic Centre, The Farm, and The Preserve are all points in the village that tell the stories of the Pleasant Hill Shakers. In the Historic Centre, you'll find more than 10,000 artifacts of the Shaker community. The Preserve is the ideal location for natural exploration through prairies, fields, and streams.

Best Time to Visit: The village is open Sunday through Saturday between 10:00 a.m. and 5:00 p.m.

Pass/Permit/Fees: Adult admission is $14 per person, children between the ages of six and 12 are $7, and seniors ages 62 and older are $10. There is also a $10 suggested donation for hikers not participating at the village.

Closest City or Town: Harrodsburg, Kentucky

How to Get There: From Harrodsburg, head north on S Main St. toward E Lexington St. Turn right onto US-68 E. In 7.3 miles, turn left onto Shakertown Rd., left onto W Lot Rd., and then the Shaker Village of Pleasant Hill is on the right at 3501 Lexington Rd.

GPS Coordinates: 37.81830° N, -84.74014° W

Did You Know? The Farm is a functioning farm with authentic structures built by the original Shakers.

Abraham Lincoln Birthplace National Historic Park

You've probably heard about the famous Lincoln Memorial in Washington D.C., but that's not the first one to honor the former U.S. President. At the Abraham Lincoln Birthplace National Historic Park, you'll find the first Lincoln Memorial and learn about how his early life in Kentucky prepared him to lead the country during the Civil War. Explore the symbolic birth cabin that replicates the one in which Lincoln was born in 1809 and the Sinking Spring that served as the water source for the Lincoln family when they were living on the land.

Best Time to Visit: The park is open year-round from 9:00 a.m. to 5:00 p.m., but the best time to visit is in the spring or fall for mild temperatures.

Pass/Permit/Fees: There is no fee to visit the park.

Closest City or Town: Hodgenville, Kentucky

How to Get There: From Hodgenville, head northwest toward N Lincoln Blvd. Exit the traffic circle onto US-31E S/S Lincoln Blvd. Turn right onto Park Main Entrance to reach 2995 Lincoln Farm Rd.

GPS Coordinates: 37.53171° N, -85.73555° W

Did You Know? There are 56 steps leading to the first Lincoln Memorial, which represent each of Lincoln's 56 years. Sixteen windows in the memorial and sixteen rosettes on the ceiling represent the fact that Lincoln was the 16th U.S. President.

Casey Jones Distillery

The Casey Jones Distillery is named for the master prohibition still maker, Casey Jones, who supplied moonshine and stills from Golden Pond to various notorious historical figures, including Al Capone. Jones was a legendary still maker in The Land Between the Lakes area and built copper-only stills that would produce the best-tasting moonshine in the region. Jones's stills were built with a torch, snips, hammer, soldering iron, and crimping pliers and were simple to set up or move. The last still, built in 1967 by Jones's grandson, is on display at the Casey Jones Distillery.

Best Time to Visit: Tours of the distillery are available daily, starting at 10:00 a.m. and ending at 5:00 p.m. Tours begin on the hour. Tasting is available from 10:00 a.m. to 6:00 p.m. every day.

Pass/Permit/Fees: There is no fee to tour the Casey Jones Distillery, only fees for purchases such as tastings.

Closest City or Town: Hopkinsville, Kentucky

How to Get There: In Hopkinsville, head northwest on E 9th, which turns left and becomes W 7th St. Take a slight right onto KY-91 N/Princeton Rd. and turn right onto Witty Ln. Take a left onto Distillery Rd. to reach 2815 Witty Ln.

GPS Coordinates: 36.91367° N, -87.55487° W

Did You Know? Casey Jones refused to build stills with steel even though it cost less, because it was coated with zinc, a potentially lethal alloy.

Hopkinsville Brewing Company

As the first and only craft beer brewery in the city of Hopkinsville and the county of Christian, Hopkinsville Brewing Company provides visitors with various craft beers that are brewed in the downtown Hopkinsville nano-brewery. Only 2.5 barrels of each beer are brewed at a time, making this small-batch beer truly a one-of-a-kind experience. Established in 2016, the brewery expanded quickly, and the space next door to the brewery was purchased in 2019 to offer more space for guests to sample their beverages. The brewery's goal is to provide the community with a social space in which to relax, interact with others, and learn about the craft of brewing beer.

Best Time to Visit: The brewery is open Monday through Thursday from 4:00 p.m. to 9:00 p.m., Friday from 2:00 p.m. to 10:00 p.m., and Saturday from 12:00 p.m. to 10:00 p.m.

Pass/Permit/Fees: There is no fee to visit but be sure to bring some money for beer samples.

Closest City or Town: Hopkinsville, Kentucky

How to Get There: In Hopkinsville, head northeast on S Main St. and take a right onto E 5th St. to reach the brewing company at 102 E 5th St.

GPS Coordinates: 36.86844° N, -87.48732° W

Did You Know? While you can find Hopkinsville Brewing Company beers in some local restaurants, the best place to taste them is in the taproom at the brewery.

Jeffers Bend Environmental Center

A one-acre lake, several gardens, and 2.7 miles of hiking trails await visitors to the Jeffers Bend Environmental Center. The center is on the same site as the Hopkinsville Water Treatment Plant, which provides visitors with many opportunities to study environmental topics such as water quality, soil conservation, soil science, agriculture, trees, wildlife habitat, recycling, birds, and more. The first garden at the center was planted in 2002 using labor from the Christian County Jail and is now flourishing with 100 trees, 100 shrubs, and a variety of flowers and grasses. Since then, more gardens have been added, one of which is the Community Garden, which was established to provide fresh vegetables to several nonprofits that run food distribution programs in the area.

Best Time to Visit: The best time to visit the Jeffers Bend Environmental Center is in the spring when the flowers are in bloom.

Pass/Permit/Fees: There is no fee to visit the center.

Closest City or Town: Hopkinsville, Kentucky

How to Get There: In Hopkinsville, follow N Main St. and turn right onto Metcalfe Ln. to reach the center at 950 Metcalfe Ln.

GPS Coordinates: 36.87827° N, -87.47146° N

Did You Know? The lake is host to numerous community events such as the annual *Take Kids Fishing* and *NatureFest*.

Pennyroyal Area Museum

Formerly the Hopkinsville Post Office between 1915 and 1967, the building that now houses the Pennyroyal Area Museum remains untouched since it was built in the early 20ᵗʰ century. The Pennyroyal Area Museum was the first museum in Hopkinsville and currently is the only museum in the city that is dedicated to displaying historical items that feature Edgar Cayce and African American history. The museum is part of a group of museums called the Museums of Historic Hopkinsville Christian County. In addition to the Edgar Cayce Exhibit and the African American History Exhibit, the Pennyroyal Area Museum also has a permanent Military Exhibit.

Best Time to Visit: The museum is open Tuesday through Saturday from 10:00 a.m. to 4:00 p.m. Since the museum is indoors, it is comfortable to visit year-round.

Pass/Permit/Fees: There is no fee to visit the Pennyroyal Area Museum.

Closest City or Town: Hopkinsville, Kentucky

How to Get There: In Hopkinsville, head southeast on E 9ᵗʰ St. toward S Virginia St., and the museum is on the right at 217 E 9ᵗʰ St.

GPS Coordinates: 36.86554° N, -87.48709° W

Did You Know? Check out the miniature circus that may have been the inspiration for Robert Penn Warren's *Circus in the Attic*, and the Charles Jackson circus collection, in the Pennyroyal Area Museum.

Ruff Park

This 49-acre park in Hopkinsville features a dozen lighted tennis courts, several open game field areas, eight baseball fields, playgrounds, a rugby field, and the large Herb Hays covered pavilion, which can be reserved and rented for gatherings. The Hopkinsville YMCA youth baseball program uses the facilities at Ruff Park for its practices and games. Numerous community events are also held at Ruff Park, including fireworks shows for the Fourth of July, Movies in the Park, and various fairs and festivals. This park is a particular favorite of tennis players, as they can access the courts at any time of the day or night when the park is open.

Best Time to Visit: Ruff Park is open year-round, but the best time to visit is during the spring or fall when the weather is mild.

Pass/Permit/Fees: There is no fee to visit Ruff Park.

Closest City or Town: Hopkinsville, Kentucky

How to Get There: From Hopkinsville, head northwest on E 9th St., which turns left and becomes W 7th St. Turn right onto North Dr., left onto Litchfield Dr., and then left again to reach Ruff Park.

GPS Coordinates: 36.88512° N, -87.49304° W

Did You Know? In 2020, Ruff Park was damaged by an E-F1 tornado. "Sparkling Ice" stepped up to restore the baseball fields with a Major League Baseball-like field coating to help the community heal from the devastation.

Trail of Tears Commemorative Park and Heritage Center

Located on land that was once used by the Cherokee tribe, the Trail of Tears Commemorative Park and Heritage Center memorializes the tragedy of the Indian Removal Act of 1830, when Native Americans were forced to leave their lands to reside on reservations. During the arduous walk, many Native Americans died, and two of their gravesites were located in this park. The gravesites of Chief Fly Smith and Chief White Path are two of the few verified gravesites along the trail. You can also visit the log cabin Heritage Center that contains numerous Native American artifacts and there are areas where you can have a picnic while you reflect on the complicated history of this area.

Best Time to Visit: The park is open all year, but the Heritage Center is only open in the summer, on Tuesday through Saturday, from 10:00 a.m. to 2:00 p.m. (after June 3, it extends its hours to 4:00 p.m.).

Pass/Permit/Fees: There is no fee to visit the trail.

Closest City or Town: Hopkinsville, Kentucky

How to Get There: In Hopkinsville, head southeast on E 9th St. In 1.4 miles, turn left onto Trail of Tears Dr. to reach the trail at 100 Trail of Tears Dr.

GPS Coordinates: 36.85432° N, -87.47010° W

Did You Know? While close to 12,000 Cherokee Native Americans began their journey on this trail, only 10,500 arrived safely in Indian Territory.

Ashland - The Henry Clay Estate

Ashland is the former home of the renowned American attorney and statesman Henry Clay, who, while born in Virginia, began his legal career in Kentucky. He served as Secretary of State for President John Quincy Adams between 1825 and 1829. Clay considered Ashland his refuge and sanctuary from his difficult career and was one of the few places where he felt content. He purchased the land for Ashland in 1804, having lived in Lexington since 1799. After his death in 1852, Ashland was eventually bought and restored by his son James in honor of his father.

Best Time to Visit: Tours are available Tuesday through Saturday from 10:00 a.m. to 4:00 p.m. and on Sunday from 1:00 p.m. to 4:00 p.m.

Pass/Permit/Fees: Adult admission is $25, and students between the ages of six and college-age are $15. Children ages five and under are free.

Closest City or Town: Lexington, Kentucky

How to Get There: In Lexington, head southeast on Ave of Champions. Continue onto Euclid Ave. and take a slight left onto Fontaine Rd. Turn left onto Sycamore Rd., turn right onto Fincastle, and then turn left to reach the estate at 120 Sycamore Rd.

GPS Coordinates: 38.02914° N, -84.48167° W

Did You Know? Henry Clay's great-granddaughter Nannette McDowell Bullock established the Henry Clay Memorial Foundation to preserve the land as a museum.

Aviation Museum of Kentucky

This museum that honors aviation history in Kentucky is located at the Blue Grass Airport in Lexington. It opened in 1995 with 20,000 square feet dedicated to exhibits, a library, and an aircraft repair and restoration shop. The permanent collection in the museum holds photographs, historic aircraft, documents, and training equipment, much of which was donated by members of the Kentucky Aviation History Roundtable, which is a group of aviation enthusiasts who originally conceived of the idea to create a permanent museum at the airport.

Best Time to Visit: The museum is open Tuesday through Saturday from 10:00 a.m. to 5:00 p.m. and on Sunday from 1:00 p.m. to 5:00 p.m.

Pass/Permit/Fees: Admission to the museum is $10 for adults, $8 for seniors ages 60 and over, and $6 for children ages six to 16. Children under the age of six are free.

Closest City or Town: Lexington, Kentucky

How to Get There: In Lexington, follow S Limestone and turn left onto W High St. Continue onto Versailles Rd. and then use the left two lanes to access Man O War Blvd E. Turn right onto Airport Rd. to reach 4029 Airport Rd.

GPS Coordinates: 38.03429° N, -84.59851

Did You Know? Both military and civilian aircraft are on display in accordance with the museum's mission of celebrating the entirety of aviation history.

Central Public Library of Lexington

The Central Public Library of Lexington opened in 1905, incorporating the collections of the Lexington Library Company and the Transylvania Library, both of which were established in the late 18th or early 19th centuries. The building where the library is located is known for its rose-colored granite façade, large windows, and the lobby rotunda. From the first floor of the rotunda, you can look up and see all five floors and the world's largest ceiling clock with Foucault pendulum. There is also a mural on the ceiling that depicts the history of the horse in the Bluegrass Region.

Best Time to Visit: The Central Public Library of Lexington is open Monday through Friday from 10:00 a.m. to 6:00 p.m. and Saturday from 9:00 a.m. to 1:00 p.m.

Pass/Permit/Fees: There is no fee to visit the library.

Closest City or Town: Lexington, Kentucky

How to Get There: In Lexington, follow S Upper St. and turn right onto Bolivar St. Turn left onto S Broadway and then continue onto Harrodsburg Rd. Turn right onto Beaumont Centre Pkwy. and left onto Fieldstone Way to reach the library at 3080 Fieldstone Way.

GPS Coordinates: 38.04617° N, -84.49676° W

Did You Know? The library's Kentucky Room is where you'll find census records for the state, along with resources for researching genealogy and local history.

Headley-Whitney Museum

This art museum opened in 1966 as a private gallery to display the personal work of jewelry designer George Headley III. Two years later, he opened the gallery's Jewel Room and Library to the public. Eventually, more rooms were opened, with the full museum having been completed in the 1970s. The museum now includes the Jewel Room, the Bibelot, the Library Collection, the Shell Grotto, the Marylou Whitney Rose Garden, and the Whitney Estate Dollhouses. The museum is named after its benefactors. The Bibelot room was initially designed to replicate a jewelry box with rosewood doors and brass finishing. The Library is home to George Headley's collection of 1,500 volumes of fine art books and some of his art collections.

Best Time to Visit: The museum is open Friday through Sunday from 10:00 a.m. to 4:00 p.m.

Pass/Permit/Fees: Adult admission is $10, and children ages 12 and under are free.

Closest City or Town: Lexington, Kentucky

How to Get There: From Lexington, use S Jefferson St. to reach Old Frankfort Pike. Stay on Old Frankfort Pike for 3.5 miles after the traffic circle, turn right, turn left, and then the museum is at 4435 Old Frankfort Pike.

GPS Coordinates: 38.09730° N, -84.61057° W

Did You Know? The Marylou Whitney Rose Garden was added to the museum in 2004 as an anniversary present and is designed to replicate her garden in Saratoga, NY.

The Dr. Thomas Hunt-Morgan House

Once known as Hopemont, the Dr. Thomas Hunt-Morgan House is located in Lexington and is famous for being the home of John Wesley Hunt, the first millionaire west of the Allegheny Mountains, and Dr. Thomas Hunt Morgan (John Wesley Hunt's grandson), the first person from Kentucky to win the Nobel Prize. The house is noted for its many spectacular architectural features, such as the Palladian window in the front of the house and the lead elliptical fanlight in the entryway. The house is a product of its time, when Lexington was known as "The Athens of the West," so the Greek opulence of the house is preserved as an example of the popular Federal style in the early 19th century. You'll find an incredible collection of antiques, paintings, and early Kentucky furniture in the house.

Best Time to Visit: Tours are available Wednesday through Saturday, from 1:00 p.m. to 4:00 p.m., and from 10:00 a.m. to 3:00 p.m. on Sunday.

Pass/Permit/Fees: There is no fee to visit the house.

Closest City or Town: Lexington, Kentucky

How to Get There: In Lexington, take S Limestone to W High St. Turn right onto S Broadway, and the house is on the right at 210 N Broadway.

GPS Coordinates: 38.05105° N, -84.49608° W

Did You Know? The Alexander T. Hunt Civil War Museum is located on the second floor of the Hunt-Morgan House.

Institute 193

This contemporary art gallery was founded in 2009 in an effort to provide Kentucky and Southeastern U.S. artists with opportunities to exhibit their work, even if they haven't been considered commercially viable. Their works are chosen based on the relevance and quality of their pieces, which means more artists gain exposure than if they're chosen for their earnings potential. Institute 193's goal is to help these artists gain media attention and make connections with other artists, museums, and collectors all over the world. The museum also hosts film screenings, musical performances, lectures, and other events open to the community to foster the growth of a vibrant creative scene in Lexington.

Best Time to Visit: The museum is open Wednesday through Saturday from 11:00 a.m. to 6:00 p.m.

Pass/Permit/Fees: There is no fee to visit Institute 193, but donations are appreciated.

Closest City or Town: Lexington, Kentucky

How to Get There: In Lexington, head northwest on Ave of Champions. Turn right onto S Limestone and then left to reach the institute at 193 N Limestone.

GPS Coordinates: 38.04902° N, -84.49458° W

Did You Know? In addition to showcasing Kentucky and Southeastern U.S. artists, Institute 193 facilitates artists' events at other museums around the country.

Ironworks Pike

Also known as SR 1973, Ironworks Pike is an 18.9-mile road that passes by several Thoroughbred farms in the area around Lexington, Kentucky. Referred to as the "Horse Capital of the World," this area is the place to visit for equestrians of all ages. Even if you don't stop to visit one of the many Thoroughbred-related attractions in the area, you'll still enjoy the beauty of this drive through the Bluegrass Region. It is especially gorgeous during the fall when the leaves on the trees are changing colors or in the spring when the dogwoods are in bloom. Take tours of horse-training facilities, explore displays that tell the history of the region and sport, or simply stop beside the road to pet a horse that's wandered down from its stables.

Best Time to Visit: While Ironworks Pike offers a scenic drive at any time of the year, it's particularly beautiful in the spring or fall.

Pass/Permit/Fees: There is no fee to visit Ironworks Pike.

Closest City or Town: Lexington, Kentucky

How to Get There: In Lexington, turn right onto Newtown Pike from W Main St. In 5.7 miles, take another right onto Ironworks Pike.

GPS Coordinates: 38.12940° N, -84.47626° W

Did You Know? In April, the Horse Capital Marathon & Half Marathon is partially held on Ironworks Pike, as 98% of the race passes through rural Central Kentucky.

Jacobson Park

Jacobson Park boasts 216 acres of public space, which includes a reservoir, basketball court, dog park, open play fields, seven shelters, a sprayground, and four volleyball courts. Fishing, pedal boating, and kayaking are all popular activities on the reservoir. A two-person pedal boat can be rented for $5.30 for 30 minutes, and a four-person pedal boat or a two-person kayak can be rented for $7.50 for 30 minutes. You will also need to pay a $3.20 boat launch fee. If you bring your own non-motorized watercraft, you'll only have to pay the boat launch fee. There are several fishing docks located throughout the park, but be sure to have a valid Kentucky fishing license if you are 16 years old or older.

Best Time to Visit: The park is open year-round, but the boat dock is only open in the spring and summer and on weekends until the last weekend in October.

Pass/Permit/Fees: There is no fee except boat rentals.

Closest City or Town: Lexington, Kentucky

How to Get There: In Lexington, follow E Main St. to Richmond Rd. In 4.7 miles, turn left onto Old Richmond Rd., and then take three consecutive lefts to reach the park at 4001 Athens Boonesboro Rd.

GPS Coordinates: 37.98458° N, -84.42557° W

Did You Know? The dog park at Jacobson Park is eight acres in size and includes two paddocks (one for small dogs), benches, a tree line, and a water station.

Keeneland

Keeneland is a combination racetrack and horse auction site, making it a unique facility in the Thoroughbred industry. Horse racing events are held twice a year, and auction events are held four times a year. Trainers, owners, riders, and fans come from all over the world to participate in races and auctions at Keeneland, which has the mission of improving safety, promoting integrity, and strengthening the sport of racing. The April and October races feature 32 graded stakes that are worth over $9.6 million. More than 300,000 people attend these two races each year.

Best Time to Visit: Since there are only two races and four auctions each year, the best times to visit are in April and October for racing and in January, April, September, and November for an auction.

Pass/Permit/Fees: The fee to visit Keeneland will vary based on the event you choose and the seats you select.

Closest City or Town: Lexington, Kentucky

How to Get There: In Lexington, use S Limestone St. to turn left onto W High St. Continue onto Versailles Rd. and then turn right onto Old Clubhouse Ln. Stay on Old Clubhouse Ln. until you reach Keeneland at 4201 Versailles Rd.

GPS Coordinates: 38.04678° N, -84.60805° W

Did You Know? Keeneland operates the Keeneland Kids Club, which has more than 10,000 members and is designed to grow the racing industry.

Kentucky Horse Park

In 1777, the Governor of Virginia awarded 9,000 acres of land to William Christian as payment for his service during the French and Indian War. Christian intended to establish a farm there in 1785. However, he was killed by Indians just a year later, and 3,000 acres of his land was willed to his daughter Elizabeth Dickerson. Eventually, part of this land became the Kentucky Horse Park, which aims to celebrate man's relationship with the horse.

Best Time to Visit: The Kentucky Horse Park is open from June 2 through October 31 on Wednesday through Sunday, from 9:00 a.m. to 5:00 p.m.

Pass/Permit/Fees: Adult admission is $20 per person, and children between the ages of six and 12 are $10. Seniors ages 62 and older are $18, and children ages five and under are free. There is also a $5 daily parking fee.

Closest City or Town: Lexington, Kentucky

How to Get There: In Lexington, take W Main St. and turn right onto Newtown Pike and then left onto Iron Works Pike. Turn right onto Iron Works Pkwy. and then take the first exit at the traffic circle onto Cigar Ln. Continue onto Iron Works Pkwy. and take a left onto Wing Commander Way to reach the park at 4089 Iron Works Pkwy.

GPS Coordinates: 38.15084° N, -84.52100° W

Did You Know? The International Museum of the Horse provides 60,000 square feet of exhibitions.

Lexington Visitors Center

Located in the historic Lexington Courthouse, the Lexington Visitors Center provides expert advice from Visitor Information Specialists on the best things to do and see in the city. There are also free brochures and maps available to assist you with your visit. Plan to spend some time in the Visitors Center, though, because it also has interactive screens to teach you about the Bluegrass Region, a create-a-digital-postcard center, and several photographic opportunities, including one with a life-sized blue horse. While you're in the building, take a moment to look at the architecture of the courthouse. It was designed by architectural firm Lehman and Schmitt and is a stellar example of Richardson Romanesque design. It was used as a courthouse through 2001 but was eventually closed due to environmental issues.

Best Time to Visit: The Lexington Visitors Center is open Monday through Friday from 9:00 a.m. to 5:00 p.m. and Saturday from 10:00 a.m. to 5:00 p.m.

Pass/Permit/Fees: There is no fee for the visitors' center.

Closest City or Town: Lexington, Kentucky

How to Get There: In Lexington, follow Kentucky State Highway 922 S/Newtown Pike. Take Exit 115 and travel to N Upper Street, where the courthouse is located.

GPS Coordinates: 38.04844° N, -84.49746° W

Did You Know? The bell on the courthouse has been in all four state courthouses since 1806.

Mary Todd Lincoln House

This house, which is located in downtown Lexington, is where the future wife of President Abraham Lincoln lived as a teenager with her family. It became a museum in 1977, becoming the first house museum in the country dedicated to a First Lady. The house was built between 1803 and 1806 and was initially supposed to be an inn, but in 1832, it was sold to the Todd family. Mary Todd, born in 1818, lived in the Todd home until 1839, when she moved in with her older sister in Springfield, Illinois. While there were many outbuildings to the home when the Todds lived there, they are no longer present on the property. However, the 14-room house tells the story of a teenage Mary Todd and her life before she married Abraham Lincoln.

Best Time to Visit: The museum is open from March 15 through November 30, Monday through Saturday, from 10:00 a.m. to 3:00 p.m.

Pass/Permit/Fees: Adult admission is $15 per person, and youth admission for ages six through 17 is $6 per person. Children ages five and under are free.

Closest City or Town: Lexington, Kentucky

How to Get There: In Lexington, take S Limestone to W Main St., and the museum is on the left at 578 W Main St.

GPS Coordinates: 38.05219° N, -84.50274° W

Did You Know? The Todd family was forced to sell the property in 1849 when Mary's father, Robert S. Todd, died in a cholera epidemic.

McConnell Springs

This 26-acre park is in the center of an industrial area in Lexington. There are two natural springs: The Blue Hole and The Boils. The Blue Hole flows underground in the limestone bedrock and appears blue because of its unusual depth of 15 feet. The Boils gets its name from the appearance of boiling water when it rushes up from underground following heavy rain. The "boiling" effects can reach two feet above ground. The water of this spring and The Blue Hole is fairly cold (55°F). As the waters drain from the surface, they disappear into a cave-like formation called The Final Sink.

Best Time to Visit: The best time to visit McConnell Springs is during the spring after a major rainfall.

Pass/Permit/Fees: There is no fee to visit the springs.

Closest City or Town: Lexington, Kentucky

How to Get There: From Lexington, use S Limestone to turn left onto W High St. Turn right onto S Jefferson St., which becomes Manchester St. Continue to Old Frankfort Pike. Turn left onto McConnell Springs Rd., left onto Cahill Rd., and right onto Rebmann Ln. The springs are on the right at 416 Rebmann Ln.

GPS Coordinates: 38.05524° N, -84.52778° W

Did You Know? Two other features to see at McConnell Springs are the farm site and the bur oak, both of which are over 200 years old.

Old Frankfort Pike

Old Frankfort Pike, often referred to locally as Thoroughbred Alley, is considered one of the top 10 scenic drives in the country. Along the 16.9-mile byway that connects Frankfort and Lexington, you'll pass by numerous Thoroughbred horse farms that the Kentucky Bluegrass Region is famous for. When you're not gazing at the bucolic bluegrass fields, you'll marvel at the tree diversity in the area, as the road is lined with Osage orange, redbud, red oak, white oak, dogwood, and sugar maple trees. Back when Kentucky was considered the "wild, wild west," Old Frankfort Pike was simply known as the Old Lexington-Frankfort Road. It has roots that can be traced to the Revolutionary War.

Best Time to Visit: In spring and fall, the foliage is at its most beautiful.

Pass/Permit/Fees: There is no fee to visit Old Frankfort Pike.

Closest City or Town: Lexington, Kentucky

How to Get There: From Lexington, use S Jefferson St. to get onto Old Frankfort Pike. At the traffic circle, take the 2nd exit to stay on KY-1681/Old Frankfort Pike.

GPS Coordinates: 38.08730° N, -84.58847° W

Did You Know? Along Old Frankfort Pike, you'll pass such famous Thoroughbred farms as Frankfort Park Farm, Darby Dan Farm, Bluewater Sales, Ballantrae Farm, and Carriage Station Farm, among several others.

Old Kentucky Chocolates

This chocolate shop has been making candy in Kentucky's Bluegrass Region for over five decades. It is most famous for its Bourbon Chocolates and Bourbon Cherries, which feature 100-proof Jim Beam Kentucky Bourbon. You can even get free samples of their bourbon candies to give you a taste of what you won't be able to resist buying. Their store is open for purchases of their Old Kentucky Derby Mints, Old Kentucky Bourbon Chocolates, Chocolate Thoroughbreds, and The Colonel's Favorite Old Fashion Pulled Creams.

Best Time to Visit: Old Kentucky Chocolates is open Monday through Saturday from 10:30 a.m. to 7:00 p.m. and on Sunday from 12:00 p.m. to 6:00 p.m.

Pass/Permit/Fees: There is no fee to visit Old Kentucky Chocolates, but tours are $5 per person when available, and you'll want money for purchases.

Closest City or Town: Lexington, Kentucky

How to Get There: In Lexington, take S Limestone and continue onto Nicholasville Rd. Turn right onto Rosemont Garden and left onto Southland Dr. Turn right at Southport Dr. to reach Old Kentucky Chocolates at 450 Southland Dr.

GPS Coordinates: 38.03509° N, -84.51463° W

Did You Know? The first Bourbon Chocolate made at Old Kentucky Chocolates was in 1964, and since then, the candy company has devoted its chocolate-making process to showcasing the best of Kentucky craftsmanship.

Raven Run Nature Sanctuary

A 734-acre property, Raven Run Nature Sanctuary was acquired by the Kentucky Heritage Land Conservation Fund to give visitors the opportunity to become familiar with and appreciate more than 600 species of plants and 200 species of birds. Begin at the Nature Center, where you'll find several interactive exhibits, pamphlets about various aspects of the sanctuary, and the start of the facility's trail system. Throughout your hike, you'll come across woodlands, streams, meadows, and the remnants of 19th-century settlers. Be sure to visit the Joe Pulliam Memorial Pollinator Garden located in front of the Nature Center, which is a native plant garden that provides milkweeds, sources of nectar, and shelter to monarch butterflies during their North American migration.

Best Time to Visit: The best time to visit Raven Run Nature Sanctuary is during the spring when the flowers are in bloom, and the monarch butterflies are in the state.

Pass/Permit/Fees: There is no fee to visit the sanctuary.

Closest City or Town: Lexington, Kentucky

How to Get There: In Lexington, follow E Main St. to Richmond Rd. Take a slight right onto Old Richmond Rd. and then turn right onto Jacks Creek Pike. Stay on Jacks Creek Pike until you turn left onto Raven Run Way.

GPS Coordinates: 37.88881° N, -84.39831° W

Did You Know? There are 10 miles of trails at Raven Run, but only one, the Freedom Trail, is paved.

Red Mile Harness Track

Red Mile Harness Track, now referred to as Red Mile Gaming & Racing after undergoing a rebrand in 2015, is the second-oldest harness track in the world. Harness racing is characterized by trotting horses pulling a sulky (two-wheeled vehicle) and driver around the track. Red Mile opened in 1875 with the racing of the Great Fall Trots, and the facility has been in operation since then—over 145 years. When the facility underwent a concept change in 2015, it added gaming to its offerings by installing more than 900 gaming terminals with 138 themes. You can also watch the simulcast of other races on the 175 HD televisions located around the facility.

Best Time to Visit: The best time to visit if you want to see horse racing is during August, September, and October.

Pass/Permit/Fees: Fees vary with event and seat selection.

Closest City or Town: Lexington, Kentucky

How to Get There: In Lexington, head northwest on Ave of Champions and continue onto Winslow St., which turns left and becomes S Upper St. Turn right onto Bolivar St. and then left onto S Broadway. In 0.6 miles, take a right onto Red Mile Rd. and then a right onto Winbak Way to reach the track at 1200 Red Mile Rd.

GPS Coordinates: 38.04346° N, -84.51987° W

Did You Know? The Red Mile Harness Track hosts other events throughout the year like Family Funday and Wiener Dog Races. Check the website for the dates of these events.

The Monroe Moosnick Medical and Science Museum

Located on the campus of Transylvania University, the Monroe Moosnick Medical and Science Museum displays some of the 19th-century science artifacts, botanical paintings, and anatomical models that the university used in its medical classes between 1820 and 1850. The museum, which is named after Transylvania University Professor Monroe Moosnick, who devoted more than four decades to the collection, has curiosities on display such as a cow hairball that was donated by Abraham Lincoln's brother-in-law, fetal skeletons under glass domes, a two-headed baby, partly fleshed skulls, thousands of dead birds, and a two-faced kitten.

Best Time to Visit: Tours of the museum are by appointment only in March, April, October, or November.

Pass/Permit/Fees: There is no fee to visit the Monroe Moosnick Medical and Science Museum.

Closest City or Town: Lexington, Kentucky

How to Get There: In Lexington, get onto S Limestone and then turn left onto W 4th St. Take another left onto N Upper St. to reach the museum at 300 N Broadway.

GPS Coordinates: 38.05158° N, -84.49327° W

Did You Know? Until the doctor training school at Transylvania University closed in 1859, it was considered one of the top medical schools in the country.

University of Kentucky

The University of Kentucky is a public university located in Lexington, Kentucky. There are 12 colleges that provide students with education in fields like agriculture, law, engineering, and business and economics. The attached Chandler Medical Center educates students in medicine, dentistry, nursing, and pharmaceuticals. Students can achieve a range of degrees from the University of Kentucky, including undergraduate, graduate, and professional degrees. The university was initially chartered in 1865 as a land-grant college and was originally known as the Agriculture and Mechanical College as part of Kentucky University. The two organizations separated in 1878, and the college received university status in 1908.

Best Time to Visit: The University of Kentucky is open all year, but tours typically only occur during the school year.

Pass/Permit/Fees: There is no fee to visit the university.

Closest City or Town: Lexington, Kentucky

How to Get There: In Lexington, head northeast and turn left onto Ave of Champions. Take a left onto S Limestone to reach the university.

GPS Coordinates: 38.03089° N, -84.50479° W

Did You Know? In the 20th century, the University of Kentucky basketball team emerged as an NCAA powerhouse, winning seven NCAA championships, four of which were under longtime coach Adolph Rupp.

Waveland State Historic Site

Waveland State Historic Site is also known as the Joseph Bryan Estate and incudes three original outbuildings: a smokehouse, icehouse, and slave quarters. Tours of the mansion and outbuildings seek to tell the story of the people who lived there — the landowners and the slaves who worked the land and in the house. Bryan's grandfather, William Bryan, married Mary Boone, one of Daniel Boone's sisters. Joseph Bryan, Mary Boone's grandson, inherited Waveland and built the mansion in the mid-1840s. On his plantation, he ran a gunsmith shop, a gristmill, a paper mill, a blacksmith shop, and a distillery.

Best Time to Visit: The museum is open for tours Wednesday through Saturday, between 10:00 a.m. and 4:00 p.m., and on Sunday from 1:00 p.m. to 4:00 p.m.

Pass/Permit/Fees: Adult admission is $12 per person, children between the ages of six and 12 are $6 per person, and seniors ages 62 and older are $10 per person.

Closest City or Town: Lexington, Kentucky

How to Get There: In Lexington, head northwest on Ave of Champions and continue onto Winslow St., which turns left and becomes S Upper St. Continue onto S Limestone, then Nicholasville Rd. In 4.2 miles, turn right onto Waveland Museum Ln.

GPS Coordinates: 37.97162° N, -84.53664° W

Did You Know? Joseph Bryan grew tobacco and hemp on his plantation land.

West Sixth Brewing

This brewery is situated in a 100-year-old building known as the Bread Box. More than 30 types of beer, which are sold at various marketplaces, are brewed every year out of West Sixth Brewing. You can also experience these brews at the brewery's taproom. The brewers focus on creating small batches of craft beer that have a positive impact on the community. One of their most popular lines is their County Series, which is a group of beers named after 14 counties in Kentucky.

Best Time to Visit: The main brewery and taproom are open Sunday through Tuesday from 11:00 a.m. to 10:00 p.m., on Wednesday and Thursday from 11:00 a.m. to 11:00 p.m., and on Friday and Saturday from 11:00 a.m. to 12:00 a.m.

Pass/Permit/Fees: There is no fee to visit West Sixth Brewing, but money is required for purchases.

Closest City or Town: Lexington, Kentucky

How to Get There: From Lexington, head northwest on Ave of Champions. Turn right onto S Limestone and left onto W High St. Take another right onto S Broadway, left onto W 6th St., and then right onto Bellaire Ave. to reach the brewery at 501 W 6th St. #100.

GPS Coordinates: 38.06007° N, -84.49205° W

Did You Know? West Sixth Brewing is heavily involved in the community through its foundation, the Sixth for a Cause Foundation.

Windy Corner Market

The Windy Corner Market sells only local goods such as Larry Marks honey, jams, nut butter, tea, coffee, hot sauces, flours, soaps, and much more. It's an excellent place to shop for a Kentucky-made item to bring back home as a souvenir. You can even get a hand-curated, pre-assembled gift basket designed by Windy Corner Market owner Ouita Michel. Attached to the market is a restaurant that proudly serves meals made with the products sold in the market. Some of their specials include Po-Boy sandwiches, Stone Cross Farm Sausage Biscuits, Windy Corner Hot Brown, and Fried Sweet Banana Pepper Rings.

Best Time to Visit: The Windy Corner Market is open seven days a week.

Pass/Permit/Fees: There is no fee to visit the market, only to purchase wares.

Closest City or Town: Lexington, Kentucky

How to Get There: From Lexington, head northwest on Ave of Champions and then turn right onto S Limestone. Continue onto Old Paris Rd., and then take a slight right onto Paris Pike. Turn right onto Muir Station Rd. to reach the market at 4595 Bryan Station Rd.

GPS Coordinates: 38.10505° N, -84.37611° W

Did You Know? Windy Corner is designed to resemble an old-fashioned country store that exudes the hospitality of a small town in America.

Levi Jackson Wilderness Road Park

A heap of history and fun awaits visitors at Levi Jackson Wilderness Road Park. You can explore Kentucky's pioneer past by visiting McHargue's Mill, a reproduction of a grist mill that might have been on the banks of the park's river more than 200 years ago. You can walk in the footsteps of early settlers by taking a hike along a section of the Wilderness Road that pioneers like Levi Jackson used to reach Kentucky from Virginia. In 1775, Daniel Boone entered Kentucky through the Cumberland Gap, creating the Wilderness Road, a rough and steep trail through the mountains that originally could only be accessed by foot or on horseback.

Best Time to Visit: The park is open all year, but it's best visited in the mild temperatures of spring or fall.

Pass/Permit/Fees: There is no fee to visit Levi Jackson Wilderness Road Park, but some activities, like the Treetop Adventure, swimming pool, or mini golf, may require a separate fee.

Closest City or Town: London, Kentucky

How to Get There: From London, take S Main St. to S Laurel Rd., and then turn left onto State Hwy 1006 to reach the Levi Jackson Wilderness Road Park.

GPS Coordinates: 37.08422° N, -84.05480° W

Did You Know? Levi Jackson's partner, John Freeman, received the park's land as payment for his service in the Revolutionary War.

Van Hook Falls and Cane Creek Valley

Located in the Daniel Boone National Forest, Van Hook Falls and Cane Creek Valley are part of the Cane Creek Wildlife Management Area. If you're looking for a hike that leads to a picturesque spot where you can relax and enjoy a picnic, this is your trail, since the large slabs of rock around Cane Creek create ideal spots for sitting along the banks of the water. After lunch, continue along the trail to Van Hook Falls, which is a 40-foot waterfall that plummets vertically into Cane Creek. The entire hike (out and back) is about five miles, and you can either stick to the paved trail that will take you around a lake or trek through the woods, which provides a more scenic walk. Since the trail is right next to the creek, it can get wet and slippery after rain, so take caution as you hike to the falls.

Best Time to Visit: Spring is the best time to visit the falls, especially after rain because the falls will be fuller.

Pass/Permit/Fees: There is no fee to visit Van Hook Falls and Cane Creek Valley, but there is a $3 per vehicle, per day fee to visit the Daniel Boone National Forest.

Closest City or Town: London, Kentucky

How to Get There: From London, use E 5th St. to turn right onto KY-192 W. In 14.5 miles, the trailhead is on the right.

GPS Coordinates: 36.99853° N, -84.28510° W

Did You Know? In the spring, numerous smaller waterfalls are viewable on this hike.

Conrad-Caldwell House Museum

Often referred to as Conrad's Castle, the Conrad-Caldwell House Museum is one of the best examples of Richardsonian Romanesque architecture in the country. It was one of the first houses in the area to feature electric lighting and indoor plumbing. Its magnificent architecture features seven types of hardwoods, gorgeous stained-glass windows, fierce-looking gargoyles, and much more. Two of the city's most famous businessmen, Theophile Conrad and William E. Caldwell, lived in the house, and the opulence reveals their lavish lifestyles.

Best Time to Visit: The museum is open Wednesday, Friday, Saturday, and Sunday from 12:00 a.m. to 4:00 p.m.

Pass/Permit/Fees: Adult admission is $10 per person, students with ID are $6 per person, and seniors ages 65 or older are $8 per person. Self-guided tours on Wednesdays are $5 per person, regardless of age.

Closest City or Town: Louisville, Kentucky

How to Get There: In Louisville, use I-65 S to take exit 135 toward St. Catherine W. Keep left at the fork and follow the signs for S 1st St. Turn right onto E St. Catherine St. Turn left onto S 3rd St., right onto W Magnolia Ave., and left onto St. James Ct. to reach the museum at 1402 St. James Ct.

GPS Coordinates: 38.22978° N, -85.76333° W

Did You Know? The house became a boarding home for female students in 1944.

E.P. "Tom" Sawyer State Park

This 550-acre state park is located on the land where the former Central State Hospital once stood. There are many opportunities for sport and activity in the park, including 12 tennis courts, three lighted softball fields, 14 soccer fields, a 1.25-mile nature trail, a dog park, playgrounds, a permanent BMX track, a public archery range, the largest outdoor swimming pool in the city, a splash park, a model aircraft airfield, and picnic facilities. You'll also find the Urban Astronomy Center, operated by the Louisville Astronomical Society, situated in the park. The dog park has three two-acre plots: one for dogs under 30 pounds and two others for all dogs. You do need to be a member of the Louisville Dog Run Association to use the dog park.

Best Time to Visit: This park is open year-round, but the pool and splash park are ideal in the summer months.

Pass/Permit/Fees: There is no fee to enter E.P. "Tom" Sawyer State Park, but there are fees to participate in some individual activities like the swimming pool.

Closest City or Town: Louisville, Kentucky

How to Get There: From Louisville, follow I-71 N and take exit 9A for I-265 W, and then exit 32 for KY-1447 W. Turn left onto Freys Hill Drive, and the park is on the right.

GPS Coordinates: 38.28807° N, -85.55508° W

Did You Know? The park is named for Erbon Powers "Tom" Sawyer, father of journalist Diane Sawyer.

Farmington Historic Plantation

Farmington Historic Plantation was constructed in 1816 for slaveowners John and Lucy Speed. This 550-acre property grew hemp and was worked by almost 60 African American slaves who lived in cabins around the plantation. Abraham Lincoln visited the Speeds in 1841, and he forged a relationship with John and Lucy's son, James Speed, who would eventually become Lincoln's Attorney General. Even though the Speed family believed in emancipation and they were abolitionists, they accepted slavery as a way of life for agricultural success.

Best Time to Visit: The house is open Tuesday through Friday from 10:00 a.m. to 4:00 p.m. and on Saturday from 11:00 a.m. to 1:00 p.m.

Pass/Permit/Fees: Adult admission is $10 per person, and children are $5 per person. Seniors and military members are $9 per person.

Closest City or Town: Louisville, Kentucky

How to Get There: From Louisville, take I-65 S to exit 131A for I-264 E toward Watterson Expy. Use exit 16 to reach US-31E/US-150/Bardstown Rd. In 0.3 miles, follow a slight left onto US-150 W, and then turn right onto Wendell Ave. Take another right onto Farmington Access Rd., and the plantation is at 3033 Bardstown Rd.

GPS Coordinates: 38.21540° N, -85.66811° W

Did You Know? The plantation is host to various special events such as themed feasts and festivals.

Frazier History Museum

Previously named the Frazier Historical Arms Museum, the Frazier History Museum is an affiliate of the Smithsonian Institution and is dedicated to preserving historical artifacts dating from 1492. Its collections consist primarily of cannons, guns, daggers, swords, arrows, and artifacts from various wars. The museum is the starting point of the Kentucky Bourbon Trail, which is a tour that is designed to promote bourbon tourism in Kentucky. In 2018, the museum sold one of the most mature bourbons ever bottled — "Final Reserve: James Thompson and Brother Bourbon."

Best Time to Visit: The museum is open Monday through Saturday from 10:00 a.m. to 5:00 p.m. and on Sunday from 12:00 p.m. to 5:00 p.m.

Pass/Permit/Fees: Adult admission is $14 per person, and children between the ages of five and 17 are $10. Seniors ages 60 or older and military members are $12. Children ages four and under are free.

Closest City or Town: Louisville, Kentucky

How to Get There: From Louisville, take I-64 west for 47.9 miles to W River Rd. Take Exit 5B and travel for 0.7 miles to W Main St. The museum is on the right at 829 W Main St.

GPS Coordinates: 38.25846° N, -85.76443° W

Did You Know? Guests can experience bourbon tastings at the Frazier History Museum for an additional fee.

Kentucky Museum of Art and Craft (KMAC)

Phyllis George, a former first lady of Kentucky, established the Kentucky Art and Craft Foundation in 1981 as a way to celebrate and increase interest in the state's long, storied history in crafts. Eventually, this foundation led to the collection of American Folk Art from various locations around the region. Eventually, in 2001, the Kentucky Art and Craft Foundation became the Kentucky Museum of Art and Craft and secured a physical location in a four-story structure in downtown Louisville. The three galleries on the first three floors of the building provide 27,000 square feet for large art exhibitions. In 2016, the museum underwent a rebranding to become KMAC to better reflect its purpose of fostering creative thinking and exploration.

Best Time to Visit: The museum is open Wednesday through Sunday from 10:00 a.m. to 5:00 p.m.

Pass/Permit/Fees: Adult admission is $6, and seniors ages 65 and older are $5. Children and students are free.

Closest City or Town: Louisville, Kentucky

How to Get There: In Louisville, take W Liberty St. to S 5th St. Turn left onto W Main St. to reach the museum at 715 W Main St., which is on the right.

GPS Coordinates: 38.25813° N, -85.76171° W

Did You Know? The museum is host to various events throughout the year, including KMAC Couture, Martinis & Mistletoe, and KMAC Poetry Slam, among many others.

Kentucky Science Center

The Kentucky Science Center is considered a leader in inquiry-based learning for its numerous interactive exhibits throughout its three floors of space in a historic building on Louisville's Museum Row. It offers daily programming for visitors of all ages and science-themed films on a giant four-story movie screen. The center began in 1871 as a cabinet full of curiosities in the Public Library System of Kentucky but has evolved into the area's leading place for science education. Originally called the State Science Center, the facility was rebranded in 2012 as the Kentucky Science Center to better reflect its history of providing STEM education to all audiences.

Best Time to Visit: The center is open daily from 9:30 a.m. to 5:00 p.m.

Pass/Permit/Fees: Adult admission is $22 per person for both the exhibits and the movie, and $17 per person for children between the ages of two and 12.

Closest City or Town: Louisville, Kentucky

How to Get There: In Louisville, use W Liberty St. to turn right onto S 5th St. Turn left onto W Main St. and then take two rights to park. To reach the center at 727 W Main St., you'll need to take a stairway down to Level -1.

GPS Coordinates: 38.25836° N, -85.76266° W

Did You Know? The center hosts various special events such as *No Limits Family Nights* for children with special needs and *Eat, Drink, & Do Science* for adults.

Louisville Metro Hall

As the center of Louisville's government, the Louisville Metro Hall is the current home of the Jefferson County Clerk's Office and the Mayor's Office. Construction on the hall, which was to be used as a courthouse, began in 1837 and was in use by both governments by 1842. Designed by architect Gideon Shryock, the hall was intended to feature a six-column Doric portico, additional wing porticos, and a cupola. However, Shryock resigned in 1842, and Albert Fink, a bridge engineer, took over. He reduced the number of columns and entirely removed the cupola and additional porticos. The building was not completed until 1860. In the 1840s, the courthouse was used for slave trading, but there were anti-slavery speeches held in the hall as well.

Best Time to Visit: Louisville Metro Hall is open Monday through Friday from 8:30 a.m. to 4:30 p.m.

Pass/Permit/Fees: There is no fee to visit the hall.

Closest City or Town: Louisville, Kentucky

How to Get There: From Louisville, follow W Liberty St. and turn left onto S 4th St. Turn left onto W Jefferson St., and the hall is on the right at 527 W Jefferson St.

GPS Coordinates: 38.25559° N, -85.75951° W

Did You Know? When Frankfort was chosen to be the state capitol instead of Louisville, Louisville Metro Hall became known as "Guthrie's Folly" after James Guthrie, the Kentucky former U.S. Secretary of the Treasury who lobbied for the hall to become the state's capitol building.

Louisville Slugger Museum & Factory

The Louisville Slugger Museum & Factory is where baseball fans can see a Major League Baseball bat created. Originally called the "J.F. Hillerich Job Turning" company, in 1864, it focused on making spindles, shutters, and other practical wood items. However, J.F. Hillerich's son, John Andrew "Bud" Hillerich, was an amateur baseball player and used the factory to make baseball bats for himself and his teammates. By 1884, Pete Browning, star player of the Louisville Eclipse, commissioned 17-year-old Bud to make a bat for him.

Best Time to Visit: The Louisville Slugger Museum & Factory is open Monday through Saturday from 9:00 a.m. to 5:00 p.m. and Sunday from 10:00 a.m. to 4:00 p.m.

Pass/Permit/Fees: Adult admission is $16 per person, and children between the ages of six and 12 are $9 per person.

Closest City or Town: Louisville, Kentucky

How to Get There: In Louisville, take W Liberty St. Turn left onto S 4th St. and left onto W Jefferson St. Take a right onto S 7th St. and then turn left onto W Main St. The museum is on the left at 800 W Main St.

GPS Coordinates: 38.25824° N, -85.76372° W

Did You Know? Bud's father wanted nothing to do with making bats, thinking there was no money in baseball, but Bud continued to improve his bats until, in 1897, his father agreed to change the name of the company to Louisville Slugger after Browning's team nickname.

Louisville Zoo

Formally named the Louisville Zoological Gardens, the Louisville Zoo boasts 134 acres of animal exhibits that feature more than 1,700 animals. The zoo opened in 1969 when it had just 250 animals on display, including mostly four-legged animals like elephants and giraffes. Since that day, the zoo has continued to add amenities, such as a fully restored Philadelphia Toboggan Company carousel in 1997 and the Glacier Run Splash Park in 2007. Currently, there are six animal zones to visit, which are The Islands, Glacier Run (featuring polar bears), South America, Africa, Australia, and HerpAquarium.

Best Time to Visit: The zoo is open March through September from 10:00 a.m. to 5:00 p.m. and in October through February from 10:00 a.m. to 4:00 p.m.

Pass/Permit/Fees: Adult admission ranges between $14 and $24.95; children ages three to 11 and seniors over the age of 60 range from $9 to $19.95 depending on the day. Children under the age of two are always free.

Closest City or Town: Louisville, Kentucky

How to Get There: In Louisville, take I-65 S to exit 131A to get onto I-264 E. Then take exit 14 to get onto KY-864 N/Poplar Level Rd. Turn right onto Trevilian Way, and then take another right to reach 1100 Trevilian Way.

GPS Coordinates: 38.20651° N, -85.70721° W

Did You Know? In 2003, the Gorilla Forest received the Association of Zoos and Aquariums award.

Mega Cavern

The Mega Cavern is a man-made underground facility that was once the home of Louisville Crushed Stone, a massive limestone quarry. Over a period of 42 years in the 20th century, miners blasted out enough rock to fill 4,000,000 square feet of space. In 1989, the quarry was acquired by private investors to create an environmentally friendly, high-security commercial storage facility. There are still plans to create this storage space, but since that will only make a small dent in the amount of space available, a portion of the cavern is available for tours. There are walking or bike tours available, but the most popular tour is the Mega Tram, which drives through portions of the cavern and makes stops to explain the engineering and geological features.

Best Time to Visit: The tram tours are available daily from 12:00 p.m. to 6:00 p.m.

Pass/Permit/Fees: Fees depend on the activity you select.

Closest City or Town: Louisville, Kentucky

How to Get There: In Louisville, take I-65 S to exit 131A for I-264 E. Use exit 15 to get on KY-864 N/Poplar Level Rd. Turn right onto Taylor Ave. to reach the cavern.

GPS Coordinates: 38.20227° N, -85.70410° W

Did You Know? The Mega Cavern passes under all ten lanes of the Watterson Expressway (I-264), and this area was quarried before the highway was constructed in the early 1930s.

Muhammad Ali Center

The Muhammad Ali Center celebrates the life of champion boxer and Kentucky native son, Muhammad Ali. The center tells the story of Ali's amazing life and the six principles that drove his purpose. Founded in 2005, the center not only includes exhibits but also develops public programming aimed to pass on Ali's legacy. Some programs that are offered through the center include Daughters of Greatness, The Greatest Give Back, Stories of Ali, Red Bike Moment, and many more. The center focuses on continuing Ali's humanitarian impact on communities of need by using its capabilities as an agent of change.

Best Time to Visit: The center is open Wednesday through Sunday from 12:00 p.m. to 5:00 p.m.

Pass/Permit/Fees: Adult admission is $14 per person, students with ID and military members are $10, children between the ages of six and 12 are $9, and seniors ages 65 and older are $13.

Closest City or Town: Louisville, Kentucky

How to Get There: In Louisville, use W Liberty St. to turn left onto S 4th St. Take a slight left onto N Fourth St. and then left onto W River Rd. Turn left onto N 6th St. The center is on the right at 144 N 6th St.

GPS Coordinates: 38.25912° N, -85.75988° W

Did You Know? The Muhammad Ali Center has won numerous awards, including TripSavvy Editor's Choice Award for "Best for Sports Fans" in 2019.

Speed Art Museum

The Speed Art Museum offers modern architecture, interactive exhibits, welcoming outdoor spaces, and abundant programming opportunities for people of all ages. The name "Speed Art Museum" comes from the founders' philosophy that everyone should be able to create their own art experiences and connections at their own speed. Permanent collections at the museum include Black Artists Matter, Art of Ancient Cultures, African Art, Native American Art, and European, among others.

Best Time to Visit: The museum is open Friday from 1:00 p.m. to 8:00 p.m. and Saturday and Sunday from 10:00 a.m. to 5:00 p.m.

Pass/Permit/Fees: Adult admission is $20 per person, and children between the ages of four and 17 and seniors ages 60 and older are $14. Children ages three and under are free.

Closest City or Town: Louisville, Kentucky

How to Get There: In Louisville, from S 1st St., merge onto I-65 S toward Nashville. Take exit 134 for KY-61 S/Arthur St. Turn right onto E Brandeis Ave. to E Cardinal Blvd. Take a left onto S 3rd St., and then another left to reach the museum at 2035 S 3rd St.

GPS Coordinates: 38.21867° N, -85.76094

Did You Know? Through 2024, everyone who visits the Speed Art Museum on Sundays can visit for free in honor of Owsley Brown II.

The Kentucky Derby at Churchill Downs

Churchill Downs is one of the most famous horse racetracks in the world and is known as the "Home of the Kentucky Derby." The Derby, which is the first event of the three that make up horse racing's coveted Triple Crown, is the longest continually running sporting event in the country. The facility is 147 acres in size and features a one-mile oval dirt track. Over 165,000 guests come through the gates each year. The twin spires atop the grandstand are the facility's most recognizable architectural feature and were designed by architect Joseph Dominic Baldez. Museum tours are available daily, but live racing is only available during select months of the year, including the first Saturday in May when the Kentucky Derby is held.

Best Time to Visit: The only time to visit the Kentucky Derby is on the first Saturday in May every year.

Pass/Permit/Fees: The fee to visit the Kentucky Derby at Churchill Downs will depend upon seat selection.

Closest City or Town: Louisville, Kentucky

How to Get There: In Louisville, get onto I-65 S and take exit 132 for Crittenden Dr. Turn right onto Central Ave., and then take two lefts to reach the track at 700 Central Ave.

GPS Coordinates: 38.20443° N, -85.77257° W

Did You Know? The Kentucky Derby is known as the most exciting two minutes in sports because of the approximate time it takes to determine a winner.

Louisville Palace Theatre

Located in Louisville's downtown commercial district, Louisville Palace Theatre originally opened in 1928 and is the only movie house in the city from this time that survived urban renewal. Initially called the Loew's and United Artists State Theatre, the architecture received rave reviews from numerous newspapers and magazines of the time. The theatre flourished throughout the 1970s as a first-run movie center, and then in the 1990s, investors began restoration that would result in the renovated Louisville Palace. The 2,800-seat theatre has an opulent interior with a distinctive Spanish design. The theatre continues to screen films, but it also hosts numerous live events as well. The Marquee Lounge is an exclusive bar just for premium seat holders, where they can enjoy a drink and appetizers prior to the show.

Best Time to Visit: The best time to visit The Louisville Palace is when there is a show you want to see.

Pass/Permit/Fees: Rates will vary based on the production and your seat selection.

Closest City or Town: Louisville, Kentucky

How to Get There: In Louisville, use W Liberty St. to turn right onto S 3rd St. Turn right onto W Muhammad Ali Blvd. and left onto S 4th St. to reach the theatre at 625 S 4th St.

GPS Coordinates: 38.24830° N, -85.75789° W

Did You Know? The Louisville Palace can be rented out for private events and can accommodate up to 2,500 guests.

Thomas Edison House

This house was the home of Thomas Edison when he was working as a telegraph operator for Western Union in 1866. While he didn't live here long, it was as a telegraph operator that he became fascinated with inventions, and many of his early inventions involved the telegraph. In fact, throughout his life, Edison received over 125 patents related to the telegraph. The house is a shotgun duplex, which is a design in which all rooms are located in single file for the length of the structure. Artifacts you'll see in the house include the cylinder phonograph, the disc phonograph, and an Edison Kinetoscope.

Best Time to Visit: The museum is open for tours on Tuesday through Saturday, from 10:00 a.m. to 2:00 p.m.

Pass/Permit/Fees: Adult admission is $5 per person, students are $3, and seniors ages 60 and older are $4. Children ages five and under are free.

Closest City or Town: Louisville, Kentucky

How to Get There: In Louisville, from W Liberty St. turn left onto S 2nd St. Turn right onto W Market St. and then left onto S Clay St. Turn right at the third cross street onto E Washington St., then take a left to reach the house at 729 E Washington St.

GPS Coordinates: 38.25633° N, -85.73845° W

Did You Know? While in Louisville, Edison taught himself Spanish and changed his way of writing to increase his speed as a telegraph operator.

Thoroughbred Park

Thoroughbred Park is a tribute to the history and sport of Thoroughbred horse racing. Across 2.75 acres, there are 12 Gwen Reardon bronze statues that tell the story of the sport and include one of the greatest Thoroughbred stallions of the 1800s, Lexington. Other sculptures depict frolicking foals, seven horses racing, and two champion horses finishing neck-and-neck at the finish line. There are five major sections of the park, each of which displays lifelike vignettes from the sport of racing. The park itself is dedicated to the horse named Lexington, who was America's leading sire for 16 years despite being blind since he was five years old.

Best Time to Visit: Thoroughbred Park is open all year.

Pass/Permit/Fees: There is no fee to visit the park.

Closest City or Town: Lexington, Kentucky

How to Get There: From Lexington, take I-64 east for 41.8 miles to Kentucky State Highway 151 S in Franklin County. Take Exit 48 and travel for 14.5 miles to Woodford County. Take Exit 72A and drive for 12.0 miles to Midland Avenue in Lexington, where the park is located.

GPS Coordinates: 38.04249° N, -84.49047° W

Did You Know? Sculptor Gwen Reardon originally carried the sculpture of Lexington around in her car, hoping to find a buyer. She finally met Alex Campbell, chairman of the Triangle Foundation, who liked the statue so much he commissioned her to sculpt the remaining pieces.

Barren River Lake

Barren River Lake is a 10,000-acre body of water located in Barren River Lake State Resort Park. Anglers are attracted to the lake for its abundant populations of crappie, walleye, bass, catfish, and bluegill, and others come to relax at Sunset Beach Cove or play golf on the par-four championship course. If you don't have your fishing gear with you, it can be checked out for free at the front desk or recreation office. Boat rentals are also available, or you can keep your watercraft in one of the 100 open slips or 40 covered slips. A public boat launch is also accessible for easy access to the lake. If you want to explore the resort further, there are basketball courts, hiking trails, orienteering courses, picnic areas, playgrounds, and a shuffleboard court for guest use.

Best Time to Visit: Summer is the best time to visit.

Pass/Permit/Fees: There is no fee to visit the lake.

Closest City or Town: Lucas, Kentucky

How to Get There: From Lucas, use State Hwy 1318 to reach US-31E S. Turn right onto KY-252 N and then onto Hwy 517/Bailey's Point Rd. to reach the lake.

GPS Coordinates: 36.88266° N, -86.09857° W

Did You Know? The Barren River, named for the treeless fields lining its banks, was a historic westward route for early pioneers. Native Americans purposely cleared the area to create grasslands to draw in grazing buffalo.

Cumberland Gap National Historical Park

Located at the border of Kentucky, Virginia, and Tennessee, the Cumberland Gap National Historical Park was created to preserve a natural split in the Appalachian Mountains that allowed travelers to cross more easily from the east into Kentucky. Known as the "Mountain Gateway to the West," this route through the mountains has been traveled by buffalo, Native Americans, and American settlers for hundreds of years. Along with hiking through the gap or along 85 miles of other hiking trails, you can take guided tours of Gap Cave and the Hensley Settlement, both of which are located within the park.

Best Time to Visit: For the best views of the tri-state area, visit in the spring or fall.

Pass/Permit/Fees: There is no fee to visit the park, but camping rates vary.

Closest City or Town: Middlesboro, Kentucky

How to Get There: From Middlesboro, take US-25 E S to get on US-58 E. In 2.5 miles, make a U-turn at State Rd. 694 to reach the park at 91 Bartlett Park Rd. You will pass over two state lines to reach this park.

GPS Coordinates: 36.60073° N, -83.67001° W

Did You Know? Along the Cumberland Mountains, you can hike to the Tri-State Point, which allows you to be in three states at the same time.

Newport Aquarium

Located directly across the Ohio River, the Newport Aquarium provides visitors with the opportunity to see thousands of exotic aquatic animals, including penguins, white alligators, sharks, and stingrays. There are also several activities available such as Shark Bridge, which allows you to walk on a rope bridge just inches above a tank full of sharks, and the *Shipwreck: Realm of the Eels* exhibit that allows you to explore a sunken ship and the mysterious aquatic creatures that call the sunken ship home. At Stingray Hideaway, you can even touch a stingray or two and discover how their rubbery skin keeps them safe in the ocean.

Best Time to Visit: The Aquarium is open daily from 9:00 a.m. to 7:00 p.m. (8:00 p.m. on Saturday and Sunday).

Pass/Permit/Fees: Adult admission ranges from $22.95 to $34.99, depending on the day you visit. Child admission (ages two through 12) ranges from $14.99 to $26.99, also depending on the date you visit.

Closest City or Town: Newport, Kentucky

How to Get There: In Newport, head northeast on W 5th St. and turn left onto Monmouth St., which becomes 3rd St., to reach the aquarium at 1 Levee Way.

GPS Coordinates: 39.09523° N, -84.49749° W

Did You Know? The Newport Aquarium opened in 1999 and has received several awards, including the Number 1 Aquarium in the 2012 Readers' Choice Travel Awards.

Carter Caves State Resort Park

In 1981, Carter Caves and Cascade Caves were joined to create a state park, 146 acres of which were designated as a nature preserve to protect the Indiana bat, Canada yew, and mountain maple. In its entirety, the park encompasses 945 acres, which were privately owned for nearly 200 years until they were donated to the Commonwealth of Kentucky in 1946. Several cave tours of Cascade Cave, Saltpetre Cave, Bat Cave, and X-Cave are available, but the latter two are only open in the summer to prevent white-nose syndrome in bats. There are also more than 30 miles of hiking trails throughout the park, taking visitors to seven natural bridges, Smokey Valley Lake, and Tygarts Creek. There are also numerous non-commercial caves in the area, with Laurel Cave being the most visited when it's open in the summer months.

Best Time to Visit: Since many of the caves are only open in the summer, that is the best season to visit Carter Caves State Resort Park.

Pass/Permit/Fees: There are no fees to tour these caves.

Closest City or Town: Olive Hill, Kentucky

How to Get There: From Olive Hill, use US-60 E to reach KY-182. Turn left onto Ic-8024A to reach the caves.

GPS Coordinates: 38.36921° N, -83.12525° W

Did You Know? During the War of 1812, Saltpetre Cave was mined for potassium nitrate (saltpeter) to make gunpowder for the soldiers to use in battle.

Grayson Lake

This reservoir is 1,500 acres in size and was created in 1968 when the U.S. Army Corps of Engineers dammed the Little Sandy River. It is a popular location for camping and picnicking, and there is even an 18-hole championship golf course in the park for those who don't want to participate in water activities. Fishing boats and pontoon boats are available to rent at the on-site marina, and a free boat launch allows you to access the lake with your own watercraft. Anglers enjoy this spot because it is stocked with ample numbers of catfish, crappie, smallmouth bass, largemouth bass, and bluegill. If you don't have your fishing equipment with you, it can be checked out for free at the Campground Ticket Both. You do need to have a valid Kentucky fishing license to fish on Grayson Lake, either from a boat or the shore.

Best Time to Visit: Summer is the best time to visit.

Pass/Permit/Fees: There is no fee to visit Grayson Lake, but there may be fees for individual activities like golf and camping.

Closest City or Town: Olive Hill, Kentucky

How to Get There: From Olive Hill, follow KY-986 for 15 miles. Turn right onto KY-7 S to reach Grayson Lake.

GPS Coordinates: 38.22372° N, -83.00455° W

Did You Know? The area that is now Grayson Lake was once a popular camping spot for the Cherokee and Shawnee Native American tribes.

Bluegrass Music Hall of Fame & Museum

If you love bluegrass music, don't skip the Bluegrass Music Hall of Fame & Museum in Owensboro. This museum's purpose is to preserve the history of bluegrass music and is located just a few miles from where Bill Monroe, the "Father of Bluegrass," grew up. Along with various interactive exhibits, you'll also enjoy jam sessions, concerts, lessons, and special events. If you're in town in mid-September, get tickets for ROMP Fest, a four-day celebration of bluegrass music that's held at the Bluegrass Music Hall of Fame Museum. There is never a day that offers the same activities at the museum, so be sure to check out the website for current information.

Best Time to Visit: The museum is open Tuesday through Saturday from 10:00 a.m. to 5:00 p.m. and Sunday from 1:00 p.m. to 5:00 p.m.

Pass/Permit/Fees: Admission to the museum is $12 for adults, $10 for seniors and active military members, and $8 for children between the ages of six and 18. Children under the age of six are free.

Closest City or Town: Owensboro, Kentucky

How to Get There: In Owensboro, head north on Allen St. and turn left onto W 2nd St. to reach 311 W 2nd St.

GPS Coordinates: 37.77557° N, -87.11388° W

Did You Know? There are currently 60 members of the International Bluegrass Music Association's Hall of Fame. Learn about them at the museum!

Friday After 5

With the tagline of "Where the Weekend Begins," you know you're going to have a blast at Friday After 5. This Owensboro tradition is an award-winning summer series of outdoor concerts that are held every Friday night along the riverfront. This festival features live bands, food trucks, entertainment, and family-oriented events across seven venues: the Kentucky Legend Pier, the Jagoe Home Patio Stage, The Atmos Energy Courtyard, The Kroger Street Fair, Cannon Hall, the Romain Subaru Overlook Stage, and the Holiday Inn. The Friday After 5 series began in 1997 when just four concerts were held over four weeks. The event has grown into a 16-week series that draws in visitors from the entire tri-state area and hosts more than 70,000 people every year.

Best Time to Visit: The only time to visit Friday After 5 is during the summer on Fridays beginning at 5:00 p.m.

Pass/Permit/Fees: There is no fee for any of the events at Friday After 5.

Closest City or Town: Owensboro, Kentucky

How to Get There: In Owensboro, follow W 4th St. and turn right onto E 4th St. Turn left onto Cs-1683-80/Daviess St. You'll find Friday After 5 at 101 Daviess St.

GPS Coordinates: 37.77697° N, -87.11027° W

Did You Know? The Kroger Street Fair is a family-friendly part of Friday After 5 that features contests with prizes and a different theme each week.

Green River Distilling Company

The Green River Distilling Company dates back to 1885 when J.W. McCulloch began distilling Green River Whiskey. After a fire in 1918 and then prohibition in 1920, disaster befell the Green River Distillery, and a group of family members purchased the building and equipment to create the Medley Distilling Company. It stayed in the Medley family until 2007 when it was sold to the Terressentia Corporation. In 2020, the new owners returned the distillery to its original name.

Best Time to Visit: The Green River Distilling Company is open for tours Monday through Saturday from 10:00 a.m. to 2:00 p.m. and for sipping from 10:30 a.m. to 1:30 p.m.

Pass/Permit/Fees: Tours are priced at $15 and include three samples of whiskey.

Closest City or Town: Owensboro, Kentucky

How to Get There: In Owensboro, from W 5th St., turn right onto Castlen St. and left onto W 2nd St. Turn right onto Texas Ave., right onto Ebach St., and left onto Distillery Rd. to reach the distilling company at 10 Distillery Rd.

GPS Coordinates: 37.77940° N, -87.13780° W

Did You Know? The Green River Distilling Company is the westernmost point along the Kentucky Bourbon Trail. Along with the basic distillery tour, you can take the Barrel Thieving Distillery Tour, which goes behind the scenes of bourbon whiskey production and distillery history.

Owensboro Museum of Science & History

Founded in 1966, the Owensboro Museum of Science & History is located in downtown Owensboro in a 19th-century building. Its large exhibition space allows for numerous interactive exhibits that are focused on local history. You can learn about Owensboro government by exploring the Wendell H. Ford Government Education Center or discover the connection Owensboro has with NASCAR in The Speedzeum, the museum's motorsports gallery. You can even tour a replica of a mine in The Coal Mine Gallery, where you'll learn how miners worked and lived when coal mining was a major economic driver in Owensboro.

Best Time to Visit: The museum is open Tuesday through Saturday from 10:00 a.m. to 5:00 p.m. and on Sunday from 1:00 p.m. to 5:00 p.m.

Pass/Permit/Fees: Admission for everyone over the age of two is $5 per person. Children ages two and under are free.

Closest City or Town: Owensboro, Kentucky

How to Get There: In Owensboro, head down E 4th St. and turn left onto Cs-1683-80/Daviess St. Turn left onto E 2nd St., and the museum is on the left at 122 E 2nd St.

GPS Coordinates: 37.77565° N, -87.11039° W

Did You Know? Various handcrafted items from Kentucky artists are on display at Owensboro Museum of Science & History.

Preservation Station Market & Event Center

In 2012, mother-daughter duo Deborah Coomes and Jennifer Higdon purchased the building to fulfill their dream of creating a marketplace that held antiques, vintage items, and fabulous bargains. This 39,000-square-foot space became the Preservation Station Market & Event Center that features more than 100 vendors hawking their handmade or homegrown wares. In 2017, a 100-seat restaurant opened for customers to take a break from shopping and enjoy appetizers, salads, soups, burgers, and some of the best homemade desserts in the city.

Best Time to Visit: The Preservation Station Market & Event Center is open Thursday through Sunday, between 10:00 a.m. to 5:00 p.m.

Pass/Permit/Fees: There is no fee to visit the market.

Closest City or Town: Owensboro, Kentucky

How to Get There: In Owensboro, follow W 5th St., and then turn left onto Frederica St. Turn right onto KY-81 S, and in 3.5 miles, use the first exit at the traffic circle to get onto KY-56 W. Turn right at Horrell Rd. and then turn right again to reach the market.

GPS Coordinates: 37.70194° N, -87.28843° W

Did You Know? Watch for Market Days, when the number of vendors significantly increases and the market turns into a massive social event.

Smothers Park

Formerly known as Riverfront Park, Smothers Park is the namesake of Bill Smeathers and was created in 1816 as the first park in the city. In the mid-2000s, the park received a multi-million-dollar upgrade, and the Lazy Dayz Playground has since been named the best playground in the world by Landscape Architect's Network. Other amenities in the park include the Ronald Lee Logsdon Spray Park (open between 9:00 a.m. and 9:00 p.m. as long as the weather is good), a concession stand, picnic areas, an open-air pavilion, porch-style riverfront swings, three signature fountains that produce water shows every 15 minutes, a cascading waterfall, the Shelton Memorial, and "Games on the River" (between May and September).

Best Time to Visit: The best time to visit Smothers Park is during the summer for the water activities and during the spring or fall for all other activities.

Pass/Permit/Fees: There is no fee to visit Smothers Park.

Closest City or Town: Owensboro, Kentucky

How to Get There: In Owensboro, head north on Allen St. toward W 4th St. In 0.3 miles, turn left onto W Veterans Blvd. to reach the park on the right at 199 W Veterans Blvd.

GPS Coordinates: 37.77636° N, -87.11192° W

Did You Know? The Charles Shelton Memorial, located in Smothers Park, is a tribute to the POWs and MIAs from all American wars.

The Owensboro Museum of Fine Art

This fine art museum offers three wings of art, and the facility itself is a visually stunning aspect of Owensboro's landscape. Two of the wings are on the National Register of Historic Sites. The Ryan Sculpture Park features giant bronze sculptures completed by major American artists who were commissioned to commemorate an ancient buffalo trail that early pioneers followed to the banks of the Ohio River, where they established Owensboro. In two wings of the building, you'll find the museum's permanent collection, which contains over 4,000 world art artifacts that date back to the 15th century. Temporary exhibitions change once a quarter in the third wing and have featured more than 500 exhibits since opening in 1977.

Best Time to Visit: The museum is open Tuesday through Friday from 12:00 p.m. to 5:00 p.m. and Saturday and Sunday from 1:00 p.m. to 4:00 p.m.

Pass/Permit/Fees: There is no fee to visit the museum.

Closest City or Town: Owensboro, Kentucky

How to Get There: In Owensboro, head south on Allen St. and turn right onto W 9th St/Cs-1022 to reach the museum at 901 Frederica St.

GPS Coordinates: 7.76775° N, -87.11220° W

Did You Know? Artwork that is displayed at the museum includes pieces from Pablo Picasso, among others. Twentieth Century Studio Art Glass is on display as well, from artists like William Carlson and Stanislav Libensky.

Western Kentucky Botanical Garden

Established in 1993 out of a Master Gardener's class, the Western Kentucky Botanical Garden is the realization of a dream of Dr. and Mrs. William Tyler. The couple donated about 8.5 acres to the city to begin the garden, which later grew by an acre to create a second entrance to the garden. The primary purpose of the garden is to educate the community on plant life and teach them how to grow plants in the Kentucky region. A variety of educational programs have been created to provide instruction to groups like schools, scouts, and seniors. The garden continues to grow, with a butterfly garden and an amphitheater added in 2006.

Best Time to Visit: The best time to visit is on the first Saturday of each month when admission is free.

Pass/Permit/Fees: Adult admission is $5 per person, students and youth are $1 per person, and seniors are $3 per person.

Closest City or Town: Owensboro, Kentucky

How to Get There: In Owensboro, head south on Allen St., and then turn right onto W 5th St. Turn right onto Castlen St., and then left onto W 2nd St. Turn right onto Thompson-Berry Park to reach the gardens at 25 Carter Rd.

GPS Coordinates: 37.77711° N, -87.14466° W

Did You Know? In 2006, a country doctor's office from the 1890s was moved into the Fruit and Berry Garden. It is designed to preserve the herbal medicines that were used in the late 19th century and early 20th century.

National Quilt Museum of the United States

Bill and Meredith Schroeder established the museum in 1991 to celebrate the art of quilting and fiber art. The museum displays a permanent collection of more than 600 quilts and temporary exhibits that change every 2-3 months to expose visitors to new art throughout the year. In addition to the quilting displays, the museum offers workshops to participants of all ages that are taught by some of the top quilters in the country. The School Block Challenge is a school program that challenges students to create a quilt block from three disparate fabrics.

Best Time to Visit: The museum is open Monday through Saturday between 10:00 a.m. and 5:00 p.m. and Sunday from 1:00 p.m. to 5:00 p.m.

Pass/Permit/Fees: Adult admission is $12, students are $5, and seniors ages 62 and older are $11. Children under the age of 12 are free.

Closest City or Town: Paducah, Kentucky

How to Get There: In Paducah, head northeast on Washington and turn left onto S 4th St. Turn right onto Jefferson St. and then left onto N 2nd St. The museum is on the left.

GPS Coordinates: 37.09025° N, -88.59731° W

Did You Know? The National Quilt Museum of the United States has more than 110,000 visitors each year from all 50 states and more than 40 foreign countries.

The Pikeville Cut-Through Overlook

The Pikeville Cut-Through Project was intended to relocate the railbed in Pikeville to prevent the dust from passing coal trains from infiltrating the city. Pikeville native and mayor Dr. William Hambley conceived the project in 1960, and three years later, the federal government provided $38,000 to study the feasibility of the project. It was eventually approved, and the cut-through was completed in four stages between 1973 and 1987. During the project, the Levisa Fork of the Big Sandy River was redirected to prevent annual flooding in the city and to create more space for development. Visitors can now hike to an overlook located in Bob Amos Park to get an incredible view of the cut and the city below.

Best Time to Visit: For the most spectacular views, visit the Pikeville Cut-Through Overlook in the fall, when the leaves are changing colors.

Pass/Permit/Fees: There is no fee to visit the overlook.

Closest City or Town: Pikeville, Kentucky

How to Get There: In Pikeville, head south on 2nd St., turn right onto Huffman Ave., right onto Hambley Blvd., and then continue onto Cedar Creek Rd. Turn left onto Bob Amos Dr. to access the overlook.

GPS Coordinates: 37.47335° N, -82.53797° W

Did You Know? The Pikeville Cut-Through Project is such an incredible feat of engineering that it was called "the eighth wonder of the world" by the New York Times.

Copperas Falls

The trail to Copperas Falls is an unmarked path, but it's still fairly heavily traveled, so you should be able to find it without much trouble. If you're in the parking lot on 715, the trailhead is to your left if you're facing away from the road. It is a favorite trail in the Red River Gorge because of its overgrown forest environment. You'll also come across a variety of unique rock formations along the way, and you'll need to cross a creek as well, so be prepared to get a little wet. At the end of the trail are the 40-foot Copperas Falls and the rock shelter that has formed beneath it. Even if the waterfall isn't running because it's late summer, you can and should explore the rock shelter, which offers a wonderful view back toward the trail.

Best Time to Visit: Spring is the best time to visit because it will be running after the rainy season. It may be dried up in the late summer.

Pass/Permit/Fees: There is a $3 per vehicle, per day fee to enter the Daniel Boone National Forest to access the falls.

Closest City or Town: Pine Ridge, Kentucky

How to Get There: From Pine Ridge, use KY-15 S to turn left onto KY-715 N. In 2.1 miles, turn right to stay on KY-715 N to reach Copperas Falls.

GPS Coordinates: 37.82174° N, -83.57562° W

Did You Know? There are two other waterfalls in the area that may be running depending on the time of your visit: The Sandy Arch & Falls and Big Trickle Falls.

Sky Bridge

One of the most prominent features in the Daniel Boone National Forest is the Sky Bridge, a natural sandstone arch that spans across the trail. You can hike the 0.8-mile path to the Sky Bridge and then pass both over and under it. There is a flight of 75 stairsteps to the top of the bridge, but that's the most strenuous portion of the hike. It is rated as an easy loop hike and provides a scenic journey through the forest along the Red River Gorge. Since the hike to the bridge is easy, this sandstone structure is one of the most visited in the area. Most people rarely spend longer than 30 minutes at the bridge itself, but it does offer some spectacular photographic opportunities. This relaxing hike is perfect for a quick stop during a road trip or a family hike with young children.

Best Time to Visit: Spring and fall are the best times to visit due to the blooming flowers and changing foliage.

Pass/Permit/Fees: There is a $3 per vehicle, per day fee to visit the Daniel Boone National Forest to access the bridge.

Closest City or Town: Pine Ridge, Kentucky

How to Get There: From Pine Ridge, use KY-15 S to turn left onto KY-715 N and continue to Sky Bridge Rd.

GPS Coordinates: 37.79085° N, -83.59807° W

Did You Know? The most interesting part about Sky Bridge is that it is a double arch. There is a single pillar under the arch that divides it in two.

The Appalachians

The Appalachian Mountains run through a portion of eastern Kentucky and encompass Cave Run Lake, Carter Caves State Resort Park, Pine Mountain State Resort, Breaks Interstate Park, and Jenny Wiley State Resort Park. The area is known for its various recreational opportunities such as boating, hiking, fishing, caving, paddling, and golfing. There are also hundreds of miles of ATV trails to zip along as you experience the spectacular views of the Appalachian countryside. While you're in the region, don't forget to sample some traditional Appalachian cooking to complete your Kentucky mountain experience. The area is also home to numerous museums, such as the Coal Miners' Museum and the US 23 Country Music Highway Museum.

Best Time to Visit: Water sports are best in the summer, but hiking and fishing are better in the spring or fall.

Pass/Permit/Fees: There is no fee to visit the Kentucky Appalachian Mountains, but fees will vary depending on the parks and recreation areas used to access the mountains.

Closest City or Town: Pineville, Kentucky

How to Get There: From Louisville, take I-64 east for 157 miles to W Cumberland Gap Parkway/US-25 E S in Laurel County. Take Exit 29 and travel for 33.6 miles to Pineville.

GPS Coordinates: 36.76307° N, -83.70971° W

Did You Know? The famous Appalachian Trail does not pass through Kentucky, even though part of the mountain chain does.

Auxier Ridge Trail

Visitors who want to get an overview of the Red River Gorge geological formations will want to hike the 2.1-mile Auxier Ridge Trail. At the apex of this path, you can see the Double Arch, Courthouse Rock, Haystack Rock, and Raven Rock. In fact, if you want to extend your hike, you can take the 2.25-mile Courthouse Rock Trail to the rock formation with the same name or the 0.5-mile Double Arch Trail to Double Arch. Whether you stop at the top of the Auxier Ridge Trail or another trail, you'll be surrounded by wildflowers, trees, and bushes, making the walk peaceful and picturesque. Camping is not allowed at the top of Auxier Ridge, as the trail is too narrow.

Best Time to Visit: Spring and fall are the best times to visit when the wildflowers are blooming with color or the trees are ablaze with the changing seasons.

Pass/Permit/Fees: There is no fee to visit the Auxier Ridge Trail, but there is a $3 per vehicle, per day fee to visit the Daniel Boone National Forest.

Closest City or Town: Slade, Kentucky

How to Get There: From Slade, follow KY-15 S and turn left onto Tunnel Ridge Rd. in 3.3 miles. In 3.6 miles, turn right to stay on Tunnel Ridge Rd. and the trailhead is on the left.

GPS Coordinates: 37.82067° N, -83.68102° W

Did You Know? Rock climbing is allowed on Courthouse Rock, but it can be slippery!

Gray's Arch Trail Loop

For a two-in-one experience, take the Gray's Arch Trail Loop to Gray's Arch and Waterfall. The 50-foot-high arch spans 80 feet, and one end of it extends off a cliff, forming a buttress. The waterfall, which typically only runs in the spring, comes straight off the arch into King Branch. Gray's Arch is one of the most popular sights in Red River Gorge, so it can be busy during peak hiking season. Since it is such a picturesque location, you may even see a wedding or other event taking place at its base. The hike is approximately six miles round trip and is surrounded by breathtaking views of the gorge, rock formations, wildflower fields, and more. Plan to spend at least half a day on the trail and at the arch, as it's a perfect place for a picnic and for just enjoying your surroundings.

Best Time to Visit: The best time to visit is in the spring if you want to see the seasonal waterfall.

Pass/Permit/Fees: There is a $3 per vehicle, per day fee to visit the Daniel Boone National Forest to access the trail.

Closest City or Town: Slade, Kentucky

How to Get There: From Slade, follow KY-11 N and then turn right onto KY-77 N. The trail is in 3.4 miles.

GPS Coordinates: 37.81924° N, -83.65749° W

Did You Know? It is suggested you hike this loop counterclockwise for an easier descent. Otherwise, the path can be difficult to see.

Kentucky Route 77

A 14-mile scenic road, Kentucky Route 77 is best known for the Nada Tunnel located near the middle of this drive. The Nada Tunnel was created in the early 20th century as a passage for a train that would carry lumber through the Red River Gorge. It is a one-lane, 900-foot tunnel that is dark and mysterious, at least as you enter its shadowy depths. The tunnel is referred to as the Gateway to Red River Gorge, and you'll certainly be glad it was blasted open by dynamite for you to pass through to the incredible scenery on the other side. Kentucky Route 77 follows the Red River, which is surrounded by high sandstone cliffs, towering trees, and colorful foliage, particularly if you make the drive in the fall.

Best Time to Visit: Kentucky Route 77 is open for travel all year, but the scenery will be most scenic in the fall.

Pass/Permit/Fees: There is no fee to visit Kentucky Route 77, but it does pass through the Daniel Boone National Forest, which requires a $3 per vehicle, per day use fee.

Closest City or Town: Slade, Kentucky

How to Get There: From Slade, follow KY-11 N to Kentucky Route 77 N in Menifee County.

GPS Coordinates: 37.86364° N, -83.64346° W

Did You Know? There is a rumor that the Nada Tunnel on Kentucky Route 77 is haunted by a climber who fell to his death near the tunnel.

Rock Bridge Trail

If a scenic hike is what you're looking for, then be sure to visit the Rock Bridge Trail, which is heralded as one of the most picturesque hikes in the Red River Gorge. For most of the trail, you'll hike alongside a creek, and at the end of the path, you'll find both a natural arch that spans the creek and the gorgeous Creation Falls. The trail is 1.4 miles long and is rated as moderate, mostly because it can become slippery in wet weather. Lined with dense rhododendron bushes and towering hemlock trees, hikers will feel like they're trudging through a rainforest, especially in the spring and summer. Rock Bridge, which is the arch the trail leads to, is the only arch in the gorge that crosses the water.

Best Time to Visit: The best time to visit Rock Bridge Trail is during the spring, especially if you want the waterfall to be as spectacular as it can be.

Pass/Permit/Fees: There is a $3 fee per vehicle per day to visit the Daniel Boone National Forest to access the trail.

Closest City or Town: Slade, Kentucky

How to Get There: From Slade, use Bert T Combs Mountain Pkwy E to take exit 40 for KY-15 N. Turn right onto KY-715 N and then take another right onto Rock Bridge Rd. to reach the trail.

GPS Coordinates: 37.77017° N, -83.58858° W

Did You Know? Just before you reach Creation Falls, there is a cave-like overhang along the path that is known as the "Rock House."

Bad Branch Falls

This 60-foot waterfall located in Letcher County is a true scenic treasure. The trail to Bad Branch Falls is just over a mile long, but the journey will take about 2.5 hours to complete when walking at a leisurely pace. You will walk along an old timber road that was constructed as early as 1930 and will need to climb over several small boulders. This trail is rated as moderate because it will take you along several narrow ledges and is challenging in spots. While you hike, take note of the towering sandstone cliffs, huge hemlock trees, and many intriguing rock formations. You'll hear the waterfall long before you actually see it, as its powerful flow sends echoes against the bluffs.

Best Time to Visit: This waterfall flows well all year, but it's most powerful in the spring.

Pass/Permit/Fees: There is no fee to visit the falls.

Closest City or Town: Whitesburg, Kentucky

How to Get There: From Whitesburg, take US-119 S for seven miles, and then turn left onto KY-932 E to gain access to the falls via Bad Branch State Nature Preserve.

GPS Coordinates: 37.06833° N, -82.77206° W

Did You Know? The gorge in which Bad Branch Falls is located contains one of the largest concentrations of rare species in Kentucky. There are more than 30 species of plants along the hike to the falls. The preserve is also home to Kentucky's only known nesting pair of common ravens, so be on the lookout for them during your walk.

Pine Mountain Road

This 38-mile road is located in eastern Kentucky and takes drivers over the crest of the 2,800-foot peak of Pine Mountain. The road, which passes along the Little Shepherd Trail and can be traveled by hikers, is narrow and high, which makes it a thrill for many drivers. As Kentucky's windiest road, with more than 350 curves, you'll certainly be treated to a wide variety of stunning views as you make your way to the top of the mountain, but if you're even slightly afraid of heights, you may not want to look down. The road is mostly paved, but in some areas, it is still dirt, which adds an even more challenging element to this scenic byway. There are several outlooks with limited roadside parking along the way to the peak.

Best Time to Visit: Spring or fall are the best times to see either the blooming wildflowers or the colorful leaves.

Pass/Permit/Fees: There is no fee to visit Pine Mountain Road.

Closest City or Town: Whitesburg, Kentucky

How to Get There: From Whitesburg, use KY-15 S to turn right onto US-119 S. In 41 miles, turn right onto US-421 N to reach Pine Mountain Rd.

GPS Coordinates: 37.10849° N, -82.80319° W

Did You Know? Be aware that many sections of Pine Mountain Road do not have guardrails, so if you decide to ascend this mountain road, make sure you pay careful attention to where you are relative to the edge.

116

Big South Fork National River

Located on the Cumberland Plateau, the Big South Fork National River and Recreation Area encompasses 125,000 acres along the Big South Fork of the Cumberland River. In the 18th century, the banks of the Big South Fork were settled by mining communities, including Blue Heron which has been preserved within the area. The most prominent feature of the Big South Fork National River is the gorge that has been cut through the rock beneath the plateau. The erosion throughout the years has given rise to many incredible geologic features such as towering bluffs, natural arches, and intriguing hoodoos (rock spires). Hiking, horseback riding, whitewater rafting, mountain biking, and other outdoor activities are popular in this area.

Best Time to Visit: The best time to visit is in summer.

Pass/Permit/Fees: There is no fee to visit the Big South Fork National River.

Closest City or Town: Whitley City, Kentucky

How to Get There: From Whitley City, follow US-27 S for 17.7 miles, and then turn right onto W 3rd Ave. Turn left onto TN-297 W, and the park is at 4564 Leatherwood Rd.

GPS Coordinates: 36.4793° N, -84.6501° W

Did You Know? Part of the Big South Fork National River is in the Eastern Time Zone, and part is in the Central Time Zone. While most park amenities operate on ET, some may be in CT. It is important to plan your visit ahead of time to account for this anomaly.

Natural Arch

The Natural Arch, a stunning sandstone arch, is located in the Stearns Ranger District of the Daniel Boone National Forest. The arch spans almost 100 feet and provides a spectacular backdrop. The trail to the Natural Arch begins at the north side of the picnic area. You'll pass two scenic overlooks on the hike, so be sure to stop and take some incredible photographs from two different perspectives. The trail is just one mile long and is rated moderately easy, so most skill levels should be able to climb to the arch with little difficulty. The Panoramic View Trail is a shorter path to the arch, at just 0.5 miles, or you can take the much longer Buffalo Canyon Trail, which is five miles long.

Best Time to Visit: For the most scenic photographs and views, the best time to visit is during the fall.

Pass/Permit/Fees: There is a $3 per vehicle, per day fee required to enter the Daniel Boone National Forest to access the arch.

Closest City or Town: Whitley City, Kentucky

How to Get There: From Whitley City, use US-27 N to access State Hwy 927, and then turn right in 1.8 miles to reach the Natural Arch Scenic Area.

GPS Coordinates: 38.84201° N, -84.51213° W

Did You Know? There are about 300 stairsteps along the Natural Arch Loop Trail, which makes the path somewhat challenging, but they are spread out along the trail, so you don't have to tackle them all at once.

Princess Falls

A 1.5-mile stretch of the Sheltowee Trace Trail takes hikers along Lick Creek and Cumberland River to Princess Falls, a beautiful waterfall located in Daniel Boone National Forest. While the trail to the falls is not paved, it is well-traveled and easy to follow. If you visit in the spring when the river is running full and fast, you'll see several small seasonal waterfalls along the way, but no matter when you visit, you're sure to pass numerous rock formations and a bridge on the path to the main attraction. Once you reach Princess Falls, you can climb to various vantage points to get different perspectives of the falls. Just be aware of slippery rocks so that you stay safe.

Best Time to Visit: Spring rains cause the waterfall to flow better and several seasonal falls to sprout along the trail.

Pass/Permit/Fees: There is a $3 per vehicle, per day fee to enter Daniel Boone National Forest, where the falls are located.

Closest City or Town: Whitley City, Kentucky

How to Get There: From Whitley City, take State Hwy 1651 to Poplar Springs Rd. Turn right onto KY-92 W, and then take another right onto Triple Oak Ln. to reach the falls.

GPS Coordinates: 36.72587° N, -84.54335° W

Did You Know? Princess Falls is named for Princess Cornblossom, a Cherokee Princess who was the daughter of Chief Doublehead of the Chickamauga Cherokee Tribe.

Yahoo Falls Trail

The Yahoo Falls Trail is a 4.2-mile trail that leads to the towering 113-foot Yahoo Falls, the tallest waterfall in Kentucky. The trail is mostly easy, but there are some steep metal steps that can be slippery following a rainstorm. You'll be able to pass behind the falls and explore one of the largest rock shelters in the Daniel Boone National Forest and Big South Fork National River and Recreation Area. There are also several arches in the area, including the nearby Yahoo Arch, so take some time to explore other short trails that take you past these geologic wonders. The trail to the Yahoo Falls Arch adds about 1.6 miles to your trip, but it's worth it, as this is one of the few arches in the gorge that has trees growing across its span.

Best Time to Visit: Spring is the best time to visit the Yahoo Falls Trail if you want to see the falls since it is a seasonal waterfall.

Pass/Permit/Fees: There is no fee to visit the Yahoo Falls Trail, but there is a $3 per vehicle, per day fee to visit the Daniel Boone National Forest.

Closest City or Town: Whitley City, Kentucky

How to Get There: From Whitley City, use State Hwy 1651 to turn left onto State Hwy 700. Turn right onto Yahoo Falls Rd. to reach the trail.

GPS Coordinates: 36.76837° N, -84.52370° W

Did You Know? The name "Yahoo Falls" is thought to come from the Muscogee word "Yahola."

Oscar Getz Museum of Whiskey History

Located in historic Spalding Hall, the Oscar Getz Museum of Whiskey History offers an incredible 50-year collection of whiskey artifacts that date back to pre-colonial days. You'll see hundreds of rare antique bottles, advertising signs and art, a moonshine still, and novelty whiskey containers. Along with these artifacts, you'll get to peruse documents about the American whiskey industry. There may even be the opportunity to purchase some whiskey-related memorabilia at the museum.

Best Time to Visit: Between November and April, the museum is open Tuesday through Saturday from 10:00 a.m. to 4:00 p.m. and on Sunday from 12:00 p.m. to 4:00 p.m. Between May and October, it is open Monday through Friday from 10:00 a.m. to 5:00 p.m. and on Sunday from 12:00 p.m. to 4:00 p.m.

Pass/Permit/Fees: There is no fee to visit the museum.

Closest City or Town: Withrow, Kentucky

How to Get There: In Withrow, turn left onto Nutter Dr. from Withrow Ct. Continue onto Lincoln Way and then turn left onto Templin Ave. Turn right onto N 5th St. to reach the museum at 114 N 5th St.

GPS Coordinates: 37.81197° N, -85.47126° W

Did You Know? Also located in Spalding Hall is the Bardstown Historical Museum, which provides exhibits relating to more than 200 years of local history.

Proper Planning

With this guide, you are well on your way to properly planning a marvelous adventure. When you plan your travels, you should become familiar with the area, save any maps to your phone for access without internet, and bring plenty of water—especially during the summer months. Depending on the adventure you choose, you will also want to bring snacks and even a lunch. For younger children, you should do your research and find destinations that best suits your family's needs. Additionally, you should also plan when to get gas, local lodgings, and where to get food after you're finished. We've done our best to group these destinations based on nearby towns and cities to help make planning easier.

Dangerous Wildlife

There are several dangerous animals and insects you may encounter while hiking. With a good dose of caution and awareness, you can explore safely. Here is what you can do to keep yourself and your loved ones safe from dangerous flora and fauna while exploring:

- Keep to the established trails.
- Do not look under rocks, leaves, or sticks.
- Keep hands and feet out of small crawl spaces, bushes, covered areas, or crevices.
- Wear long sleeves and pants to keep arms and legs protected.
- Keep your distance should you encounter any dangerous wildlife or plants.

Limited Cell Service

Do not rely on cell service for navigation or emergencies. Always have a map with you and let someone know where you are and for how long you intend to be gone, just in case.

First Aid Information

Always travel with a first aid kit with you in case of emergencies.

Here are items to be certain to include in your primary first aid kit:

- Nitrile gloves
- Blister care products
- Band-aids - multiple sizes and waterproof type
- Ace wrap and athletic tape
- Alcohol wipes and antibiotic ointment
- Irrigation syringe
- Tweezers, nail clippers, trauma shears, safety pins
- Small Ziplock bags containing contaminated trash

It is recommended to also keep a secondary first aid kit, especially when hiking, for more serious injuries or medical emergencies. Items in this should include:

- Blood clotting sponges
- Sterile gauze pads
- Trauma pads
- Second-skin/burn treatment

- Triangular bandages/sling
- Butterfly strips
- Tincture of benzoin
- Medications (ibuprofen, acetaminophen, antihistamine, aspirin, etc.)
- Thermometer
- CPR mask
- Wilderness medicine handbook
- Antivenin

There is so much more to explore, but this is a great start.

For information on all national parks, visit: www.nps.gov.

This site will give you information on up-to-date entrance fees and how to purchase a park pass for unlimited access to national and state parks. This site will also introduce you to all of the trails of each park.

Always check before you travel to destinations to make sure there are no closures. Some hikes close when there is heavy rain or snow in the area, and other parks close parts of their land for the migration of wildlife. Attractions may change their hours or temporarily shut down for various reasons. Check the websites for the most up-to-date information.

Made in the USA
Coppell, TX
02 August 2022